Praise for *The Hidden Power of Your Customers*

"This is the book that shows you how to R.O.C.K. your customers' world. Read it, watch your mind-set change, unlock the hidden power of your customers, and grow your business!"

—**Ekaterina Walter, Social Media Strategist, Intel**

"The twenty-first century customer has changed, they are communicating using more channels than ever, thus customer service has to change to meet this new, more involved, more demanding customer's requirements about how they want to interact with you. So take heed, don't waste time, stop reading this blurb and buy the book. You won't regret it. Seriously."

—**Paul Greenberg, Author of** *CRM at the Speed of Light, 4th Edition*

"Readers of Becky Carroll's blog Customersrock.net have long enjoyed the posts on creating a customer strategy through conversations with the objective to retain existing customers and grow their customer base. Now they have the chance to buy the book, read, and implement it without booting up their computer. eBooks exempted."

—**Shashi Bellamkonda, Director of Marketing, Network Solutions (aka Social Media Swami)**

"You can't sell something to someone who is mad, right? Yet companies expect to do this every day. They upset customers with poor customer service, and turn around and then market them with some brand promise customers know they can't keep. Becky's book is a gold mine for businesses that are interested in learning how to truly become customer-centric, reduce costs, and increase revenue profits!"

—**Dr. Natalie L. Petouhoff, Chief Strategist, Social Media, Digital Communications and Measurement, Weber Shandwick**

"Becky Carroll has redefined what customer-centrism can be, and better yet she gives you a clear and concise playbook for making it work in your company. If you wisely want to make more money from the customers you've already worked hard to get, read this book immediately and often."

—**Jay Baer, Coauthor of** *The NOW Revolution: 7 Shifts to Make Your Business Faster, Smarter, and More Social*

"Customers are the lifeblood of our businesses, and we spend lots of time and money chasing more of them. But with *The Hidden Power of Your Customers*, Becky Carroll rightfully reminds us that the most compelling way to grow our business is to put our *existing* customers at the center of it. Becky's accessible examples and insightful perspective deliver far beyond a customer service how-to, and serve as the playbook for a customer-focused culture, approach, and mind-set that today's businesses absolutely need."

—**Amber Naslund, VP Social Strategy, Radian6, and Coauthor of** *The NOW Revolution: 7 Shifts to Make Your Business Faster, Smarter, and More Social*

"The first axiom I learned as a young marketer was that it costs more to acquire a new customer than to retain an existing one. Why, then, do so many companies exhibit an indifference to their customers, especially in light of the current social media melee? Customers are talking back, whether anyone at headquarters is listening or not. Becky Carroll is an authority on customer-centric marketing, and she writes with clarity and passion. If you want to grow your company, buy this book and read it twice."

—Connie Reece, Marketing and Communications Consultant and Founder, Every Dot Connects

"The need to listen to your customers, both to what they are saying and what they are not saying, is critical to organizations across the world, across the public and private sectors. *The Hidden Power of Your Customers* provides an excellent guide for novices and experts seeking to grow their business by properly engaging with their customers. The insights, complete with clear explanations and solid case studies, ensure this is a book you will want to read."

—John F. Moore, Founder and CEO, Government in The Lab

THE HIDDEN POWER OF YOUR CUSTOMERS

Four Keys to Growing Your Business Through Existing Customers

Becky Carroll

WILEY

John Wiley & Sons, Inc.

Published by John Wiley & Sons, Inc., Hoboken, New Jersey.
Published simultaneously in Canada.

For general information on our other products and services or for technical support, please contact our Customer Care Department within the United States at (800) 762-2974, outside the United States at (317) 572-3993 or fax (317) 572-4002.

Wiley also publishes its books in a variety of electronic formats. Some content that appears in print may not be available in electronic books. For more information about Wiley products, visit our web site at www.wiley.com.

Library of Congress Cataloging-in-Publication Data:

Carroll, Becky, 1966–
    The hidden power of your customers : Four keys to growing your business through existing customers / Becky Carroll.
      p. cm.
    ISBN 978-1-118-01821-7 (cloth)
    ISBN 978-1-118-09544-7 (ebk)
    ISBN 978-1-118-09545-4 (ebk)
    ISBN 978-1-118-09546-1 (ebk)
    1. Customer services.   2. Customer relations.   3. Customer services—Management.
4. Customer relations—Management.   I. Title.
    HF5415.5.C373 2011
    658.8′12—dc22   2011007554

Printed in the United States of America

10   9   8   7   6   5   4   3   2   1

This book is dedicated to my loving husband, Dan, without whom I would have never taken the first step, and to my sons, Tim and Matt, who encouraged me all along the way. I love you.

Contents

Acknowledgments

T his book is the culmination of more than four years of thoughts, hopes, and dreams. As you can imagine, a lot of people have contributed to those dreams along the way and have helped shape this book into a reality. Unfortunately, there are many more people who have contributed than I am able to thank here, but please know that all of you have made an impact on me and on this book. You all rock!

First and foremost, I want to thank my husband Dan. You have helped me keep my eye on the end goal. Thank you for the time you spent making dinners, creating a quiet house (so I could focus), and rubbing my back at three in the morning when I was tossing and turning over the next chapter. I couldn't have done it without you and your endless support.

I also want to tell you, Tim and Matt, how much I have appreciated all of your encouragement. From making me a snack to keeping me company to understanding when I couldn't always be with you during this project—every little thing you have done meant so much to me. Thank you for being such wonderful sons.

To my parents, Jim and Linda, thank you for your countless hours helping me with my writing, with processing the edits for this book, and with your endless support. Your contributions were tremendous, and you helped me more than you know.

Cindy, Mary, Jack, and Sue: Thank you for always believing in me and for your positive words. They have kept me moving. And Pam, I am grateful for our friendship and for all the ways you have reached out and been there for me these past months.

Over the past four years there have been many bloggers who have inspired me and advanced my writing and thinking about customers.

Mack Collier, thank you for giving my blog a kick-start as part of the "Z-List" and for your kind words, then and now. Steve Woodruff and Jay Ehret, thank you for giving me the opportunity to participate in some of your blog projects, and for your prayers when I needed them. Michael Brito, CB Whittemore, Toby Bloomberg: You are all good friends and supporters. I appreciate that you are always there when I needed to talk something over or needed a panelist or radio guest! I admire you all.

A special thank you goes out to my coworkers Judy, Helen, Mark, Jaime Lee, Becky, and Doug at Verizon, as well as Lisa at Aquent. You have given me the support I needed to complete this project. Thank you for having my back!

Kudos also to the great people at John Wiley & Sons, Inc. who have been working with me on the project: Dan Ambrosio, Ashley Allison, Lauren Freestone, and the many others behind the scenes who have made this book real. Your professionalism and expertise have been invaluable.

A big acknowledgment to all of the people I interviewed for the case studies in the book, as well as the companies and people that helped connect me with them. You are all Customers Rock!-stars from my perspective, and I appreciate your willingness to share and be a part of this effort.

Finally, many, many thanks to my UC San Diego students, my San Diego social media colleagues, and my "Customers Rock!" blog readers. All of you have encouraged me in one way or another, and I am so excited to be able to share this final work with you. You all rock!

THE RISE OF THE CONNECTED CUSTOMER AND THE NEW ERA OF RELEVANCE

G ood customer service used to be one of the secrets to business success. Over time, however, what was considered "good" turned out to be not good enough. Somewhere along the way, customers became a burden, viewed by big organizations as a cost center and by smaller businesses as an inconvenience. Processes, systems, automated attendants, and technology eventually separated us from them and ... well, here we are today, wondering how it is that the very people who contribute to the overall health of our business are farther away from us than ever before.

Let me ask you a question: When you picture customer service, do you see it from the standpoint of you as a business owner or stakeholder in a company, or do you think of it from the customer perspective, where your experiences as a customer remind you of what good service is and isn't? I have to be honest, writing this brought to mind some painful experiences, when I just didn't feel the appreciation I would expect as a customer. I have a feeling it's an experience you and I share. That's the point. As customers, we can share countless stories of unpleasant encounters—and have most likely already done so with our friends and family. How many great customer service experiences can you recall, and how often did you, or do you, talk about them today?

This is the perspective you need as you look to your customers today to grow your business tomorrow. This may sound silly, but the future of business takes a personal touch.

Let me share a secret with you, a secret that will unlock the four keys to growing your business: Empathy is the connection between you and your customers. Empathy is the bridge between your customers and their peers.

I've known Becky Carroll for several years, and the message of empathy is one she has shared with us time and time again. As so many relationships begin these days, I initially "met" Becky online, through Facebook, Twitter, and blogs. In February 2008, I had a chance to see her in action at "The Customer Service Is the New Marketing Summit," hosted by GetSatisfaction in San Francisco. Becky's session was titled "Customer Experience: The Intersection of Marketing and Customer Service," and her words still echo true today.

Great—not just good—customer service is necessary for business survival. Personalized and empowering customer service, fanned by empathy, is the recipe for viral customer service, where word of mouth becomes an extension of your marketing and sales efforts.

The future of business is rooted in shared experiences. Customer experiences will be shared, and they will either be positive or negative. Not unlike the reviews we've either posted or read on Amazon, people either love or hate an interaction they've had with a company. They feel so strongly about it, they'll take to Amazon or any other review site to ensure that everyone else *feels* what they're feeling prior to making a purchase decision. Again, customer experiences will either be positive or negative, and you can bet that they will be shared.

The wonderful aspect about all this is that you get to choose which type of experience your customers will have. More important, if you can engender a positive experience for them, you can literally plug into an entirely new world of connected consumerism that extends those exchanges beyond the typical few friends they might tell either way. Nowadays, customers are connected to one another through social networks and online groups. This isn't new; what is new is the nature of these relationships and the efficiency with which information travels within and beyond inner networks of friends.

The average person is connected to 140 people on Twitter and 130 on Facebook, and even they can trigger a social effect that extends experiences beyond small cliques of friends and family. There's a new genre of customers rapidly emerging, and they're connected to not hundreds but thousands of others. The social or connected customers is your influencer. They are the gatekeepers to a more efficient and expansive network of referrals linked by shared experiences and optimized through an endless social effect that extends your value proposition beyond your reach today. Yes, that was a long sentence, but I couldn't shorten it, as doing so would have minimized the importance of what's before you.

We are embarking upon a new era of business, one that I believe represents the end of business as usual—and this is a good thing.

Customers want a few things:

- Products or services that meet or exceed their needs.
- The ability to find what they need when they need it.
- A channel by which to be heard.

What customers now bring to the table is the ability to get each of the above *with or without you*. This is your opportunity to plug in to these networks, where you can build relationships, cultivate loyalty, and learn how to adapt, all while earning greater relevance and reach. Brilliant!

Everything begins with defining the experiences you wish others to share.

There's a mnemonic spelling lesson in English most of us learned that, to this day, is impossible to forget: "i" before "e" except after "c." It can, however, be applied to much more than everyday spelling. To remember the importance of the customer, I've adapted its definition as follows:

Insight before *engagement* unless *customer* or *community* needs take immediate precedence.

With the emergence of social media, we are given not just a right to engage but a rite of passage to earn relevance.

Social networks are much more than Twitter, Facebook, Foursquare, YouTube, et al. These networks represent a potential much more transformative: that is, the democratization of information and the equalization of influence within new digital societies. Here, everyone begins at ground zero, including you, but it is how behavior evolves that introduces us to a new future of sales, service, and business. As everyday sales and service become commodities, experiences and relationships become paramount. Peers, friends, family, and experts become trusted sources to steer and filter relationships within these new landscapes.

Sharing becomes social. Decisions become social. Commerce, and ultimately service, becomes social. At the heart and soul of all of this is the very essence of your business—shared experiences connected through empathy and fortified by the desire and intention to shape them in ways that help people help you.

Take this book and use it to grow your business. More important, use it to build relationships that turn customers into advocates and advisors.

In business, as in life, you earn the relationships and, with nurture, the yield that you've earned and deserve.

Care. Guide. Connect. Learn.

—Brian Solis (@briansolis), author of *Engage!*,
digital analyst, and champion for everyday customers

A BIRD IN THE HAND IS WORTH MORE THAN YOU THINK

he Hidden Power of Your Customers will change the way you think about your customers.

Oh, you've probably heard the terms countless times before: *customer service, moments of truth, customer satisfaction, retention,* and *loyalty.* All of these have been talked about—even extolled—for a long time now. Yet the reality is this:

- Most marketing budgets focus on acquisition, while existing customers are ignored or offered worse prices than new customers— and companies hope that existing customers won't notice.
- Companies are so busy prospecting for new customers they neglect to find out whether any of their existing customers have additional needs that can be fulfilled, thus leaving money on the table.
- Organizations create "cool" social media campaigns to gain more and more followers, friends, and fans. Yet many of the individuals with whom the brands form these new "relationships" haven't bought (and may never buy) from those companies, while loyal customers and true advocates are lost in the crowd.
- Companies have drastically slashed budgets, and often the first cuts made are to initiatives focused on customer service, as they are seen as "costs" to be reduced.
- Companies don't call on their "customer loyalty" teams until faced with a situation where they have to try to save a customer. At this point, it is usually too little, too late.

1

- Businesses work so hard to have "satisfied customers" that they don't notice when another company steps in and steals their customers by making a better offer.

So, what does all this mean? In short, it's time to get back to the basics. It's time to *return to the customer*.

RETURN TO THE CUSTOMER

The idiom "A bird in the hand is worth two in the bush" comes to mind here. I like the description provided in the *New Dictionary of Cultural Literacy*: "The things we already have are more valuable than the things we only hope to get."[1]

It has been my experience that many companies spend most of their time and budget focusing on selling to *new* customers and end up neglecting their *existing* ones. This might work in the short term, but eventually these companies will find themselves losing more customers out the back door than they bring in through the front door. Additionally, the onset of social media is driving a major change in customer behaviors and habits, making it highly risky *not* to focus on existing customers. Social media has brought the customer experience to the forefront of discussions, so it is important for companies to be more vigilant than ever before.

As a result, some people will tell you that you need outstanding customer service. But customer service is not enough. You also need *marketing* that connects with your current customers. In fact, you need to consider the entire *customer experience* and support it with a *customer-centric culture*, one that promotes an equally exceptional employee experience. And, of course, you do need outstanding *customer service*.

Strengthening customer relationships has become an integral part of doing business. As mentioned, changing customer behaviors as a consequence of increased customer expectations, coupled with increased accessibility to social media tools, have put the topics of customer service and loyalty in the spotlight. Many books have been written on these two subjects over the years, and they are still popular. However, they tend to be geared to the call center and are filled with stories and anecdotes rather than real-world strategies and successful tactics.

The Hidden Power of Your Customers is not a "customer service" book. It is a book about how to focus on your current customers in such a way that you see a side of them you may not have seen before. This book will also help organizations ensure that they aren't letting go of the "bird in the hand" while pursuing those "in the bush."

WHAT IS THE HIDDEN POWER?

Businesses have forgotten about—or perhaps never fully realized—the power that existing customers and clients can wield. The allure of new customers has hidden the power of these customers from view.

- Your current customers have the power to decide whether to continue doing business with you.
- If they do continue, they have the power to determine how much money to spend with you.
- They also have the power of word of mouth to share with others what they think about you.

Lately, most of the talk has been focused on that last power—customer word of mouth—especially in the social media realm. And make no mistake, it *is* important. However, a business that wants to fully unlock the hidden power of its customers should treat the three "powers" listed as equally important. Customers can't speak highly of your company in an authentic way if they are no longer your customers!

You have a golden opportunity to grow your business through each of your existing customers, with one or more of the following results:

1. You gain additional ongoing business from each customer (the relationship lasts longer).
2. You gain additional business from each customer (up-sell or cross-sell).
3. You gain new business from others they bring to your company.

Let's begin by looking at three potential states for your business relationship with existing customers—*business is growing, business is coasting,* and *business is shrinking*—and examine what each state looks like. What are its benefits (or detriments)? What are some strategies for increasing business growth in each area?

Business Is Growing

There are five ways to *get more business* from your existing customers:

1. The customer *renews* their existing business with you: They perceive value in what they are getting, and they keep returning for more.
2. The customer *buys more* from you than before, via a *cross-sell* or an *up-sell*: You have uncovered and met new needs for this customer.
3. The customer *expands* (via a merger or acquisition, new clients of their own, or new family members) and therefore *needs to buy more*: Due to your current relationship with these customers, they think of you first.
4. The customer *refers* or *recommends* you; they become an influencer or evangelist. "Trusted advertising" takes place as *they tell others* about their great experiences with you.
5. A customer's referral *results in a new sale*: The customer successfully convinces someone else to do business with you.

Benefits

Since you've extended (lengthened and/or strengthened) your relationship with existing customers, you now have an opportunity to learn more from each of them. This, in turn, will help you improve your products and services, fine-tune the customer experience, and better target potential prospects as you use your new customer insights. The hidden power has just been multiplied!

Strategy

Do no harm! Thank and reward or recognize your customers. Partner with them. Make it easy for them to "share the love."

Business Is Coasting

There are five ways your business may be doing little more than *coasting* with existing customers:

1. The customer is *only a follower on social media*: He or she is just looking for freebies or discounts but won't ever buy from you again.
2. The customer has *tried your business—once*: There was nothing particularly good or bad about the experience, but there was also nothing that would bring the customer back (and you've made no effort to make that happen).
3. The customer is a "hostage" and has to stay with you because there are *no other options*: This could be due to a geographical issue or the fact that you're the only game in town. This customer could bolt if a competitor breaks into your market.
4. The customer is *satisfied*: He or she is not unhappy in any way, but not thrilled either. Unfortunately, satisfaction does not equal loyalty. Customers don't tell other people about brands when they are just "satisfied" with them.
5. The customer is *tolerant* or *bored*: This customer is stagnant and not motivated to buy again.

Benefits

The customers described here have connected with your business in some way, so the door has been opened. You know who they are; you have their contact information or can access them through a channel partner. Therefore, you still have the opportunity to unlock their hidden power.

Strategy

Use relevant marketing to get the attention of these "coasting" customers, to engage them. Figure out how to better meet their needs. If they interact with you, make sure to give them a great customer experience.

Business Is Shrinking

There are five ways your existing customers can cause your *business to shrink*:

1. The customer *doesn't renew*.
2. The customer *reduces the amount* he or she is purchasing with you.

3. The customer *takes his or her business elsewhere*.
4. The customer *spreads a feeling of dissatisfaction*: This could negatively affect your brand image.
5. The customer *convinces others to leave*.

Benefits/Detriments

Clearly, there aren't many benefits here. There are, however, a number of potential solutions to the problems you're facing.

Strategy

Win the customer back by using your own outreach programs or through the positive referrals from other customers' "trusted advertising." Implement service recovery; fix what went wrong, and learn from it for next time. If you can't get the customer back for whatever reason, cut your losses. Perform damage control or PR recovery, if necessary, on any bad press.

Where Is *Your* Business?

You can't leave the care of existing customers to random chance. You also can't leave the care of existing customers only to "hero" customer service personnel who excel at handling customer problems. Instead, you need to make taking care of existing customers an ongoing, proactive part of your business for everyone in your company—and that takes time, budget, and a strategy.

What is your strategy for building your business from your existing customers? This book will help you answer that question.

ANATOMY OF A "CUSTOMERS ROCK!" COMPANY

It is increasingly harder to find new customers in the face of mounting competition for their attention. As a result, many companies resort to competing on price and trying to woo customers away from competitors. But there are companies whose customers would never leave them, no matter what competing businesses offer. How do these companies earn such loyalty? By believing their customers *rock*, and running their entire business according to that principle.

"Customers Rock!" companies build a loyal fan base by spending a large portion of their marketing and advertising budgets on the "care and feeding" of existing customers. They know their customers by face and name. They empower their employees to focus on *what's* right, not on *who's* right. They ensure that every point where they interact with customers adds to the overall "brand experience." They hire customer-facing employees who have a passion for people, and they measure these employees based on whether customers return—and bring others with them. They listen to their customers *before* speaking to them; they engage them in a two-way conversation rather than just shouting advertisements at them. They treat their existing customers like *gold*. They are truly "Customers Rock!" companies.

Not all companies function this way, as we all have experienced. These "other" types of companies are, typically, more concerned about costs than customers. They treat customer service as a cost center rather than as an opportunity to hear from customers firsthand. They pass their clients from one representative to another in a constant battle to beat the call center clock. Reps talk as fast as possible to get the information across as quickly as they can. Company marketers talk but don't listen. Every customer touch point is viewed simply as a transaction instead of an opportunity to build a relationship. These kinds of companies engage in short-term thinking. They measure their businesses only on operational efficiency; they fail to focus on measuring what is important to the customer.

Which type of companies would you rather do business with: those that know their customers *rock*, or those whose customers *walk*—out the door?

BUILD ON THE "ROCK": THE FOUR KEYS TO GROWTH

This book takes the principles that make "Customers Rock!" companies successful and divides them into four sections, described here. These principles are the keys to unlocking the hidden power of your customers. Throughout the chapters that follow, you will be challenged to take a fresh look at your business. Armed with these keys, you will learn how to turn your company into a "Customers Rock!" company, one centered on the customer. You will also learn specific steps to take to grow your business from your existing customer base.

The four keys to unlocking the hidden power of your customers spell out "R-O-C-K" and are as follows:

Key One: R—Relevant Marketing

Marketing the way a customer wants to see it.

Customers are tired of being bombarded with messages. Their expectations are high—even more so for existing customers. In this day and age of rapidly advancing, readily accessible technology, customers assume companies not only know who they are but also remember enough information about them to communicate in a way that is relevant to them—at every interaction.

This section will help you look at your approach to marketing through your customers' eyes:

- Learn about your customers by listening to them.
- Understand the customer life cycle from the customer point of view.
- Utilize marketing channels properly:
  - Find out which channels your customers prefer (e.g., e-mail, social media, phone, in-person, snail-mail).
  - Create conversational marketing that enhances the customer relationship based on customers' preferences.
- Create relevant marketing content:
  - Speak with your customers using their "language."
  - Create content they care about.
  - Stay top-of-mind with existing customers.
  - Make customers feel valued.

Key Two: O—Orchestrated Customer Experience

Seeing things from the customer's perspective.

Each place where the customer and business come together has to add value—for both the customer and the business. For customers, the value needs to be something they appreciate (i.e., they need to get what they want); for the company, it needs to be something that benefits the business (e.g., it needs to grow to succeed). "Customers Rock!" companies create a strategy for providing a consistent, gratifying customer experience across the entire customer life cycle. The only way to construct this kind of seamless experience is to align all parts of the organization around the customer.

This section will prompt you to think about your company's customer interactions, and it outlines the steps to create an outstanding experience:

- Set customer expectations.
- Create consistency among touch points (including social media).
- Identify and understand your real competitors.
- Craft the right experience for your customers.
- Reinvent processes and systems you've established for the benefit of customers.
- Fine-tune the experience.
- Establish organizational alignment.

Key Three: C—Customer-Focused Culture

It all starts here.

Customer-focused companies have the desire to fulfill their customers' needs as part of their corporate DNA. Their company cultures bring different business functions together to work toward a common set of goals: (1) strengthen customer loyalty, (2) promote customer evangelism, and (3) increase company revenues. When leaders consistently support these objectives across the organization, everyone wins.

This section outlines the culture of customer service and shows you how to support it with the right metrics and employee experience:

- Develop and maintain strong company values.
- Operate according to customer-focused metrics.
- Learn how to take action based on customer data.
- Apply customer focus to social media metrics.
- Put employees first:
  - Bring in the right kinds of employees.
  - Engage and empower them to make a difference.

Key Four: K—Killer Customer Service

Consistency is the key.

A change in the behavior of today's customers necessitates a change in the way businesses think about customer service. It is no longer simply a cost center; it is now one of the main competitive differentiators for a company.

This section advises businesses on how to take their customer service to the next level and support the customer experience with each employee interaction:

- Use social media in customer service—or not.
- Take care of the little things for customers.
- Provide customer service that gets talked about, for the right reasons.
- Recover when things go wrong.
- Follow the golden rule when dealing with customers.

HOW TO READ THIS BOOK

The Hidden Power of Your Customers is outlined according to the four keys—R-O-C-K—just defined. Use these keys to help you unlock the hidden power of your customers.

The book is designed so that a variety of readers will benefit from the material it presents. For example:

- Business leaders whose companies have reached a plateau in growth and know they need to try a different approach.
- Business managers who don't understand why their companies are not growing even though they keep bringing in new customers.
- Sales teams whose members are so focused on chasing leads they forget about their existing customers.
- CEOs who want to stop the leakage of their best customers to their competitors.

- Marketing managers who scramble to keep up with customer rants via social media outlets.
- Small business owners who want to understand why their "great customer service" isn't enough.
- Customer service teams that want to create a consistent customer experience that lasts longer than the last training session.

In short, anybody who wants to build their business on their existing customers.

In addition, executives and cross-functional teams from larger enterprises will gain value either from reading the book from start to finish or from zooming in on chapters and sections that focus on where they feel their organizations have the greatest need for improvement. The case studies in Chapters 2, 4, 7, 10, and 11 will be of particular interest to this group of readers as they focus on the customer success stories of larger enterprises.

Similarly, small and midsized business leaders will find the case studies in Chapters 3, 8, 13, 14, and 15 especially useful, as they provide an in-depth look at smaller businesses that are customer-centric. That said, any company and businessperson can benefit from reading about the accomplishments described in all the "Customers Rock!" case studies featured in this book, as they were carefully chosen to highlight work from leading organizations of all sizes. Each case study is based on my personal interviews with leaders from the featured companies; other company examples cited throughout the book were either personally experienced by me or relayed to me through trusted sources.

It's Not about Someone Else

As you read this book, you may suddenly find yourself thinking, "I wish XYZ Company would pay attention to this point!" While that is great (and I urge you to send a copy of this book to XYZ Company), I want you to keep the focus on *your* business, not on those you deal with as a customer. To that end, keep this question in mind as you go through the book: "How can we improve our customer strategy so we *rock* for our customers?"

I also encourage you to read with a highlighter in hand, so you can keep track of the areas you think offer the greatest opportunity to make a positive impact on your relationship with your company's existing customers. Then go to the Web site that inspired this book, "Customers Rock!" (http://customersrock.net), where you can download an audit that will help you determine which areas you are ready to, or need to, tackle first. There, you will also find checklists, tips, and inspirational stories of other successful companies that are growing their revenues—and their positive word of mouth—from existing customers.

What about your organization? Is it nurturing current customer relationships? Does it treat customers as if they *rock*, or not? If yes, how does it demonstrate that for customers?

In thinking about those questions, you may find it's time to make some changes.

Let's *rock*.

R—RELEVANT MARKETING
O
C
K

Marketing the way a customer wants to see it.

In the past, marketing has focused on how companies can get their messages out to as many customers as possible in order to generate leads for sales or to get people to come into a retail store or visit a Web site. However, much of that marketing is now falling on deaf ears as customers are inundated with messaging nearly everywhere they go. In addition, most marketing budgets have historically been spent on acquisition; little, if any, of the budgets have been spent on retaining, delighting, and growing existing customers.

Today's marketing organization needs to take a different approach if they want to win the hearts and minds of their customers.

"Customers Rock!" companies focus on their existing customers as a key to their future success in business. They nurture their customers. They thank them. And they listen to them, then sell what best meets each customer's needs (rather than selling to reduce inventory or make commissions).

How we communicate with our customers is critical to how they view our company. Whether the communication is written or verbal, brand impressions are made at each interaction. It isn't about social media, "user-generated content," cool videos, or flashy Web sites. It *is* about relevant marketing that speaks to the *needs* of our customers.

How can we achieve this type of marketing? We have to get out, engage our customers in conversation (online or offline, at their place of consumption), learn from their feedback, and put what we learn into action within our organizations.

When we do this, we start to strengthen our customer relationships because we are offering something to them based on what we know our customers need.

Chapter 1

LISTEN TO YOUR CUSTOMER BEFORE DOING ANYTHING

L istening has become a lost art, especially from the perspective of companies today. Many organizations don't realize how necessary it is to interact differently with their customers if they want to learn what is important to them. Most customer listening today seems to take place via surveys on the bottom of a cash register receipt, on a Web site, or by phone (usually during dinner). Alternatively, some organizations turn to customer focus groups to gain insight into their customers. Although these can be useful methods of gathering customer feedback, they don't provide the best opportunity for truly *listening* to the customer. Companies usually aggregate the results of these methods into market research reports, in which the voice and sentiment of individual customers are lost. Customers don't feel that they are being heard, with good reason—in many cases, they are not.

To unlock the hidden power of your customers, it's important to first understand their needs, their satisfiers, and their thoughts about your brand and your products (as well as those of your competitors). The best way to accomplish this task is to listen to them *before* you try to figure out how to keep (and grow) their business. "Customers Rock!" companies create customer listening posts in several channels (including, but not limited to, social media); they view customer feedback as a critical part of their business, and they take action based on what they learn.

CUSTOMER LISTENING POSTS

To begin, I advocate that you spend time on a regular basis listening to your customers at the locations where they "hang out." In many cases, that could be in online forums or chat rooms, on social networks, or elsewhere in the digital universe. In the case of Walt Disney World guests, it could even be in the hot tub!

Recently, my family stayed four nights at a Disney World resort in Florida. At the end of a long day, with feet aching, we headed to the resort's hot tub by the pool to soothe our tired muscles before another day of theme park exploration. We overheard some very interesting conversations and learned a lot.

We learned which theme park to visit early in the morning and where the crowds would be. We learned which hotel restaurants to eat at and which ones to avoid (and why). We learned what other Disney guests liked, and didn't like, about each park: the rides, restaurants, shops, lines, shows—you name it, they discussed it. We were definitely influenced by this unexpected word of mouth.

What valuable information this would be for Disney! We participated in a survey at one of the theme parks; I even took the time to answer the follow-up survey I received in my e-mail. However, I couldn't help but think that Disney's team would find much more open and honest information bubbling out of their guests (pun intended) if they went to any of the company's resort hotels and listened in on conversations taking place in the hot tubs.

Of course, we can't always be where our customers congregate. If, however, we develop an understanding of where customer conversations are already taking place, we can gain valuable insight into critical locations to set up customer listening posts.

There are two main areas where customers "hang out": those locations that are part of your company's experience (your own living room, so to speak), and those locations that are outside of your company's direct touch points.

Listen in Your Own Living Room

The first set of listening posts are on your Web site, with your sales or service teams, and, if relevant, in retail outlets. All are places where customers interact with your company and complete transactions on "your turf." Listening opportunities at them could occur during face-to-face interactions and customer service interactions and through customer feedback tools.

Here are some tips for effective customer listening at these and other company-sponsored posts.

Go Talk to Your Customers

Willie G. Davidson, grandson of the founders of Harley-Davidson Motorcycles, rides with members of the Harley Owners Group (HOG) on a regular basis. Not only is he perceived as being "one of us" by customers, he also gets the opportunity to hear firsthand what customers love and what they'd like to see improved on their Harley-Davidson bikes.

Whether you do it in person at a retail outlet or brick-and-mortar location, at a customer event or conference, during a customer sales or support call with the account team, or on a cross-country motorcycle ride, meeting with and listening to customers face-to-face is *critical*. Some organizations require their professional staff, who don't often have the opportunity to deal face-to-face with customers, to spend time interacting with them, especially during major events or the holiday season. For example, they might have these staff members answer the phones, help out in the warehouse, or work in the store. Personal interaction is an excellent way for all employees to learn about their organization's customers. Ideally, all management employees should also spend time interacting with customers in this fashion *at least* once a quarter.

Connect with Your Customer Service Organization

Wherever your customers go to contact you is an ideal place to listen to them. It could be a customer service call center or a technical support department. Visit your call center, sit down with your company's customer service reps, and have a listen—and don't forget to bring your notepad! Ideally, all employees should participate in this type of listening, at least once a year. If your company's employees aren't located near the customer service organization, provide a way for them to listen to recorded customer calls.

Read Actual Customer Comments

Don't rely solely on survey results that have been aggregated into a list of the "top customer issues." The true customer voice can be lost in these types of summaries. Request that customer comments (good and bad) be included *verbatim* in any customer feedback report so that you can "hear" what your customers are saying in their own words. Then be sure to share those comments with your team. You'll find some detailed ideas on sharing this type of information later in this chapter.

Listen Where Your Customers Are

Where do your customers congregate? Needless to say, it would be more convenient for us if our customers came to our Web site and completed our feedback form there to give us input; but let's face it, they don't always share their opinions in the channels we prefer. For that reason, it is important to set up listening posts in locations that are frequented by our customers on *their* turf, both online and offline. When you interact with customers in their own setting, don't forget to listen more than you speak.

Spend Time Listening in Social Media Channels

Customers are having conversations about your products, services, and industry on social media sites. These discussions not only take place on blogs, customer forums, discussion boards, and online communities, you'll also find them scattered across multiple social networks. That is why I strongly encourage management at all levels to add some of these interfaces to your regular listening activities—for both you and for your employees. Schedule blocks of time in your planner to listen to customers via social media. Encourage your employees to spend time listening to customers conversing online. After you've listened, have your designated team respond as needed, and engage the right resources to address any issues found.

See How Customers Use Your Products or Services

Time you spend watching customers use your products or services in their "natural setting" is a fantastic way to learn about customer needs. When I worked at Hewlett-Packard (HP), we learned about the "Day in the Life of a Customer" concept. HP researchers would arrange to visit customer sites, where they would record video of a customer's employees going about their business for a day. HP would then analyze where it could help make that customer's business processes more effective and efficient. This helped HP figure out how to fit in with the customer's processes, rather than forcing the customer to adjust to HP's processes. This is not to say that you have to record your customers' every move for a day, but you can spend some time with them, at their sites, and get to know how they do business. When you do, be sure to ask your customers what you are already providing for them that works, and what you could be doing better!

Another way to experience how customers are using your products and services is to do an *ethnography study*. Also called a *field study*, this type of research involves direct, firsthand observation of subjects going about their daily activities. The HP "Day in the Life" recording is a similar type of study. Another great example is the approach Toyota took while designing its Tundra truck: Company engineers spent time with real customers in places such as logging camps, horse farms, factories, and construction sites where the truck would actually be used. This gave Toyota engineers a firsthand look at customer needs and, thus, a better understanding of how to tweak the Tundra to work the way the customers needed it to work. For example, they discovered such nuggets of customer insight as how much towing capacity was required in these environments, where to put features like the gear shifter for ease of use, and the necessity of installing larger door handles and radio controls to accommodate the fact that workers would be wearing heavy gloves.[1]

The point here is this: Sometimes there is simply no substitute for going out and spending "face time" with your customers, watching how they do what they do, in the places they do it. What might you learn about your customers if you recorded a video of them going about their daily routines? How could you improve your company's products or processes to work better for your customers based on how *they* do their jobs? These types of customer insights cannot be easily or fully described on a survey; they must be observed "in the field."

LISTEN FOR CUSTOMER FEEDBACK

In addition to setting up customer listening posts to capture insights, it is also important to create *structured feedback* opportunities. These generally fall into two main areas: feedback on individual transactions and feedback on the overall customer experience and relationship. Many mechanisms can be used to gather customer feedback; these include surveys, customer advisory panels, and customer interviews. Surveys are probably the most widely used by companies of all sizes. The following tips can help you and your company make more effective use of surveys for gathering customer feedback.

Make It Easy for Customers to Answer Your Survey

At a recent conference, I listened to a Disney Institute instructor share how the company works to remove perceived customer barriers to taking surveys in the theme park. He explained that on some days, the survey at the entrance gate to the park might ask only for a customer's zip code. However, on days when lengthier surveys are needed from park visitors, the conversation might go like this:

Disney: "Hi! Do you have some time to take our guest survey? We would need about two hours of your time."

Guest: "Uh, no, that would take up a big chunk of my day here."

Disney: "Well, how about if we take care of you for tomorrow?"

Guest: "No, I would have to change my flights, my hotel . . ."

Disney: "What if we took care of all that? Would you be willing to give us your time then?"

Now *that* is commitment to listening to the voice of the customer!

Take the Customer's Perspective

If the survey is about a product a customer has already purchased, be clear about which item it is (ideally, the customer has many of your products). If it is a survey about the customer's relationship with your company, be sure to acknowledge how long the individual has been your customer; this will help that person feel valued.

Speak the Customer's Language, Not Yours

Phrase the survey questions in terms that customers use; refrain from interjecting company lingo. If you aren't sure which terms customers are using to discuss your products, services, or industry, that's a sign that you need to do more listening.

Asking Equals Learning

Some organizations spend more time in meetings trying to *guess* what makes their customers happy than they do finding out what they want to know from the customers themselves. The best way to determine customer desires and needs is to go directly to them and ask them.

Close the Loop after an Interaction

Take the time to ask customers about their experience with your company. Did it meet their expectations? Exceed them? Fall short? This can be done by using a short Web survey, including an invitation on a receipt to take a survey, or making a quick phone call (depending on the nature of your business). This is also a good opportunity to ask customers what your company could do differently next time.

If the survey is about a recent transaction, be as specific as possible about that exchange, to help jog the customer's memory. Above all, request the customer to complete the survey *as soon as possible* after the experience. If it has been more than a few days, most customers won't remember the interaction well enough to make the survey response worthwhile. Even if the survey is primarily about the customer's experience, be sure to also ask about the product or service, as well as the customer's relationship with you. Track responses individually, if possible, so you can go back and look for trends in how certain customers respond over time—especially your most valuable customers.

Closing the loop after an interaction is a very simple way to understand customers, but it is amazing how few companies actually execute on this strategy. If the customer experience was poor, asking about it allows customers to vent and get some mental relief. Most important, companies that close the loop and follow up promptly on issues uncovered by surveys with their customers are regarded as standouts. They can more easily and quickly recover from unfavorable situations, and they often *increase* customer loyalty by working with any disgruntled customers to "win them back." According to a study by Forrester Research, 81 percent of customers who felt that a company's resolution to their problems far exceeded expectations stated that they were very likely to do business with that company again.[2] Although this level of interaction will take dedicated effort, it is still less expensive than the effort to find new customers.

Finally, if possible, tie survey results back to employee compensation for those touch points, so that staff members are rewarded for a job well done.

Follow Up When a Customer Leaves

One of the most important points of contact occurs when a customer leaves—especially if that customer is one of the organization's "best customers" (most profitable or makes the most referrals). Too many firms that lose a customer don't bother to ask why, even though that customer might be willing to share what made them want to leave. Doing so may result in discovering how to save that customer.

If your organization has recently lost some of its most valuable customers and you don't know why, put down this book right now and make some phone calls to uncover the reasons. (Go ahead; I'll wait for you to come back.)

Involve Customer-Facing Employees

Customer service and sales teams typically have the most frequent direct interaction with customers. Smart organizations realize this and ensure that customer-facing employees are an integral part of providing customer feedback and insight. They are your company's eyes and ears, and they hear more about the customer than most. Their insight is invaluable; don't miss out on it!

LISTEN FOR CUSTOMER INSIGHT

Listening for customer insight goes beyond what customers are saying on the surface; it also listens "between the lines." This leads to deeper insights about customer behaviors and, ultimately, customer needs. Some of the best insights can be gained in social media channels, where customers voice their opinions and share unsolicited feedback about brands, products, and services with their peers.

Areas to Explore

There are three key questions to consider when listening for customer insight, either via social media or traditional channels:

1. *What pain points are being expressed by your customers?* Are they voicing legitimate concerns, or just airing frustration? Never dismiss customer rants, especially on social media, as they can escalate quite quickly. Check out rants as soon as possible to ensure that an underlying issue doesn't exist. Negative comments can also help alert you to potential unmet customer needs.

2. *What emotion or sentiment is being shared, either positive or negative?* Identifying emotions will help reveal how customers feel about your brand, product, or service, as well as how they feel about related brands, products, or services. Recognizing these emotions can help your company better understand customer drivers, behaviors, and needs.

3. *What information is being shared about the various interactions in the customer experience?* Is the information about the company at large, or is something being said about a particular situation or individual? This information can help clarify customer experience details and point out potential process improvements.

Take Action on What You Hear

An important part of listening is to loop back to your customers to let them know you heard them. This should be an immediate response, if possible, especially when issues are uncovered via social media. Ideally, this is the continuation of an ongoing conversation between your company and your existing customers that will build relationships into the future.

Address Any Expressed Pain Points Promptly, Efficiently, and without Emotion

If pain points are voiced online, other customers with similar experiences can easily turn them into a series of rants. Follow up quickly with the first customer who expressed dissatisfaction, apologize for it, involve your customer service team, where appropriate, and learn from the discussion. If other customers have already begun to pile onto the initial concern, be sure to address their needs as well.

Use Insight Gained from Listening Posts to Refine Customer Needs

You may find out just as much about the behavior of customers through their verbatim language on their favorite social media sites (be it consumer- or business-focused) as you will through surveys. Feed these social media insights into your organization.

Supplement What You Learn via Social Media with Additional Primary Research

While social media can provide important customer insights, keep in mind these venues represent only a subset of your customer base. Understand which customers are using social media, and make sure to round out your findings by listening and interacting via other customer touch points and research tools.

Share the Knowledge

Customer insight is most valuable when it is shared across the organization. I once visited a company that offered virtual computing products and had a chance to see how its staff shared customer feedback. My contact there took me on a facility tour, and for me the most interesting point was when she walked me past their "Voice of the Customer Wall." On it were three large groupings of many signs, divided up according to the company's main product lines, each a different color. Each sign was a verbatim quote directly attributed to a customer. The Customer Wall was in an area near the employee break room, where it was convenient for workers to stop and, literally, read "the writing on the wall" from customers. I love this idea of making customer comments visible to all in the organization. It was inspiring to see actual customer comments displayed all over the wall in plain sight!

Do you listen to your customers often enough and well enough to get these types of quotes? It is important to share the "voice of the customer," including their verbatim comments, with the rest of the organization. Too many companies tend to hold customer information within corporate "silos." By this, I mean that individual departments are not always diligent about sharing what they know or have learned about customers with other parts of the company. This knowledge-is-power attitude cannot exist if the goal is to create a "Customers Rock!" company. *Every* employee should understand how the company's customers perceive their brand, products, and services, in the actual language used by those customers.

FOUNDATION FOR THE FOUR KEYS

Now more than ever, it is critical for companies whose goal is to be customer-centric to listen to customers across the entire experience. These companies will learn to use their understanding of customers to find ways to meet customer needs in relevant ways, through whichever touch point the customer chooses to use. Such companies will move from "influencing customers" to "collaborating with customers" through the use of ongoing, meaningful discussions—many of which may take place via social media channels. These interactions, coupled with proactive customer listening, will deepen customer relationships over time and ultimately increase customer value and loyalty.

To achieve the best results, customer listening activities should take place on a regularly scheduled basis. How often will depend on your role in the organization and how prepared your organization is to take action on what is heard. That last point bears repeating, so let me say it another way: Take decisive action based on the results of listening to your customers. Don't waste their valuable feedback and the effort it took to get it! Treat what you learn from listening to customers as a critical piece of data, along with other research findings, to help you make decisions about your products, services, and customer experiences. The insights gained from customer listening and feedback will inform the strategy for executing on the four keys to growing your business from existing customers.

So, what are you waiting for? Start listening. Get to know your customers—today!

Chapter 2

KEEP CUSTOMER NEEDS IN MIND

L istening to customers is an effective way to learn about their thoughts, feelings, and preferences regarding your industry and products or services.

How much insight do you have into the minds of your customers? Do you know their habits, actions, and language? How well? Do you take the time to understand how they interact with your products or services? Before we can take action on the information we have gathered, it's important to process what we have learned in the context of the customer. This includes developing an understanding of the customer life cycle, knowing where the customer is in the cycle, and determining customer needs and behaviors.

EXPERIENCE THE LIFE CYCLE

Consider the customer life cycle in your industry and how you address the customer experience at each stage of the cycle. Note that I am not discussing the *product* life cycle here. Nor am I discussing the customer life cycle from a *company's* point of view. Rather, I'm talking about the *customer's perspective*—experiencing the life cycle the way a customer would.

Companies tend to list four life-cycle stages: *prospecting*, *acquisition*, *service*, and *retention*, all of which are internally focused. In contrast, the five customer life-cycle stages from the customer's perspective are as follows:

1. *Research*: Everything customers learn about whether a product or service can meet their needs, from searching the Internet, reading company Web sites or collateral, reviewing ratings and reviews, asking friends and colleagues for recommendations, reading blogs, and seeking expert opinions.
2. *Purchase*: Everything customers go through to buy the product or service and take it home or to their place of business.
3. *Usage*: Everything customers do to start and continue using the product or service, including setup and installation, ongoing use of the product or service, and getting help when things go wrong or a question arises.
4. *Repurchase*: Everything customers do to buy the product or service again, including renewals, buying from the same company, or switching brands or suppliers.
5. *Retirement or disposal*: Everything customers go through to dispose of the product or service, including returning equipment, recycling, or selling the product to someone else.

As customers move through these five life-cycle stages, their satisfaction, loyalty, and advocacy may change, based on their experiences with the company and with the product or service. In addition, if this is a business customer, needs will likely change based on the company's business stage (is this a start-up or an established company?). Therefore, it is essential to understand the customer's current business stage in order to be the most relevant to that customer's needs.

UNDERSTAND THE CUSTOMER'S STATE OF MIND

The customer life cycle begins with personal or business needs. Next, customers look for products and services that will help them meet those needs. That said, there are many facets to understanding what each individual customer needs; moreover, needs may vary depending on the life stage of that customer. For individual consumers, this may be similar to the myriad stages of life: student, single, married/divorced, and so on. For a business customer, this may vary depending on either the stage of the company (start-up, growth, acquisition, decline, bankruptcy) or on an employee's needs and roles within the company (C-level, line of business, admin, human resources, purchasing, and so on).

In addition, a customer's perception of a brand may change based on what they intend to do at the moment, as well as on the goals they want to achieve by making their potential purchase. Their needs may also vary depending on the reason they're seeking out a given product or service. This is where we can start to group our customers into "segments" based on what drives their behavior.

To begin, we must consider that all customers are not created equal. For example, let's examine the needs of customers who are searching for a restaurant. One set of customer needs might require a quiet environment that is conducive to conversation, a diverse menu that includes low-cal choices, and availability of their favorite wines. Another group of customers might be looking for a more fun-filled atmosphere where they can party with friends, listen to good music, and buy inexpensive but delicious food.

These two sets of needs may not necessarily be based on customer demographics; they may depend on whether the restaurant is being chosen for business or recreation purposes, to meet budgetary constraints, to host a holiday or birthday party, or just for personal preference. Ideally, companies must understand the many factors that spark the needs of their existing customers so they can begin to anticipate what any particular customer might need at any given time.

MEET THE NEEDS OF YOUR CUSTOMERS

The role of marketing in an organization today is significantly changing. It is no longer enough to "push" a product or service at a customer, believing it will meet that individual's needs because that customer fits into a certain demographic. I might, for example, purchase a printer for my computer so I can print e-mail messages and business documents, whereas someone else might purchase it to print digital photos for a scrapbook. Both of us might be of a similar age and have a similar income and education, but clearly this information is not enough to ascertain how each of us will use the printer.

Likewise, knowing which magazines a consumer subscribes to, which TV shows they watch, and what kinds of car-care or cleaning products they purchase doesn't really tell you the whole story either. It is, therefore, critical that marketers understand customer needs on a deeper level, based on what *motivates* customers to make certain choices; marketers must understand the underlying drivers of customer behavior.

To achieve this deeper understanding of the needs of each customer, marketers are finding it necessary to view their company, its products and services, and each place a customer "touches" their company from the customer's perspective.

Become a Customer Needs Expert

Marketers can no longer rely solely on traditional methods they've used in the past to understand customer needs. For example, focus groups used to give marketers an idea of customer direction, or a general understanding of behaviors. In practice, however, we may not really understand what individual customers need without listening to each of them and asking them different types of questions. To continue with the printer example: Why is *this* customer purchasing a printer? Have they ever purchased one before? What do they need from a printer? Better yet, what task are they trying to accomplish—and how much of that could be facilitated by the printer? Digging as deeply as possible into the reasons behind customer needs and behaviors is a critical function—and one that not many sales teams or marketers are performing well.

Gather Big Insights

A great example of understanding customers comes from one of my favorite movies, *Big*. This film, which stars a young Tom Hanks, is about a 12-year-old boy who magically becomes a 30-year-old man overnight and ends up working for a toy manufacturer. One of the things I like about the movie is its view of the corporate marketing world as seen through the eyes of a boy in the body of a man.

In one memorable scene we find Hanks's character, Josh, in an FAO Schwarz store (a very hands-on toy store). The CEO of the toy company,

Mr. MacMillan, is also in FAO Schwarz to observe how kids are playing with the toys there. When he sees Josh in the store and recognizes him as an employee, the two start talking. Mr. MacMillan realizes that this young man has a very different perspective from most of the other young professionals working at his company. As the two watch kids playing with the toys in the store, they talk about what they are seeing. Here is part of the interchange:

MacMillan: I come down here every Saturday. You can't see this on a marketing report.
Josh: Um, what's a marketing report?
MacMillan: Exactly.[1]

When Hanks was preparing for the role, he watched tapes of his costar, David Moscow (who plays Josh at age 12), to see how he behaved and acted. The director of the movie, Penny Marshall, also filmed each grown-up scene with Moscow playing the part of Josh so Hanks could see how a 12-year-old might handle that situation. The result gives true insight into the mind of a young boy.

We can learn a lot from the MacMillan character. This fictional executive spent time at a retailer watching how his customers interact with various toys in order to learn more about the people who buy them. Notably, in the movie, he promoted Josh to a job where Josh's keen understanding of customer needs could be fully utilized. This is similar to Willie Davidson's objective to understand his customers' needs more fully by riding a Harley-Davidson motorcycle with them, described in Chapter 1. Some things you just can't see on a marketing report.

Marketing teams must view their companies through the eyes of their customers if they want to become customer needs experts in this new customer-centric business world. To accomplish this important task, marketers have to do more than just watch tapes of focus groups and read survey results; they must intimately get to know customer wants, needs, frustrations, and raves.

At this juncture, we can begin to segment customers based on what we have learned. One product or service offering may appeal to different people for different reasons. For example, a racing video game might appeal to people who like the realism of the cars in the game. Others may enjoy the game because they love the feeling of driving fast. Still others might like to play it because it is fun and helps them bond with their families or forget their workday. Smart marketers work to understand which of their existing customers fit into each of these "segments" and tune their marketing messaging to match these specialized needs.

When Nintendo was creating its Wii gaming system, the company was pitted against two other console manufacturers with large customer bases. The coveted customer was the so-called hard-core gamer, and Nintendo's competitors attracted most of that segment. So Nintendo decided to change the game (pun intended) by understanding the needs of other potential gamers.

Nintendo's game developers started by listening to the company's existing customers. When they asked them why they played video games, one of the top reasons always cited was "to have fun." Is this really a surprise? Thus, when the Nintendo developers were designing the Wii, they kept this simple fact in mind—to keep video games fun. Where many of the video games developed for hard-core gamers required a steep learning curve, which discouraged the "average" gamer, Nintendo made the wise decision to design the Wii as a fun, innovative console that belonged in the center of the living room, not the back bedroom. Nintendo's primary focus was on improving the *customer experience for the average gamer*, instead of making it better, faster, and flashier for the elite group of hard-core gamers.[2]

Ultimately, any company's goal should be to craft the optimal customer experience at each stage of the customer life cycle, taking the stage and needs of the customer into account *at each interaction*. In Nintendo's case, through talking to existing customers, Nintendo learned that they could not only focus on meeting the needs of existing video game buyers but also use what they learned to create a fun experience for their friends and family as well. Whether your customers interact with you through a Web site or a video game console, ask yourself what you can do for them to help them meet their needs or achieve their goals.

To craft the optimal customer experience, it is imperative that companies put a repeatable system in place to *collect* customer information, to create a method for *sharing* that information throughout the organization, and finally, to *act* on the information. Learning from our customers, then using what we have learned to improve the customer experience, is a good way to defend against customer attrition. When we use the information that we have gained to do something different for each customer based on that customer's needs, we offer a unique value proposition for our customers, one our competitors can't match. We are able to use customer insight that they don't have. And when we continue to learn from each future interaction, and adjust our behaviors accordingly to benefit our customers, we strengthen each customer relationship and, ultimately, build loyalty.

Grow the Business

As marketers begin to understand customer needs more deeply, they can create campaigns that are more relevant, better customized, and more likely to spur engagement with the brand. This should result in increased action (i.e., more business with the company) on the customer's part.

When an organization remembers the customer's previous interactions and uses that "corporate memory" to improve the customer's experience the next time, it is building trust with its customers. Trust and corporate memory lead to relevant marketing; they are critical components in forging solid relationships with, and ensuring loyalty from, existing customers. And, of course, growing business from existing customers is one of the most cost-effective approaches to success there is!

Right-Selling versus Up-Selling

I read an interesting article in the *New York Times* on "Scientific Selling," which started with the following sentence: "The way in which a customer is handled has much to do with results obtained." How true that is! The article went on to discuss how a customer cannot be "up-sold" unless that customer is thoroughly understood. "The worst evil in selling is the action of the man who merely gives the customer what he asks for. The man who does this is not a salesman, he is just a clerk."[3]

Printed almost 90 years ago, on June 18, 1922, those statements still ring true today. We need to understand not only who our customers are and what they want but also how they are currently using our products and services. The most satisfied customers tend to be those who are using the products and services that provide the best fit for their needs.

When I was at HP, I worked in the division that marketed service subscriptions for the company's mainframe computers to businesses. The subscription included software updates and the ability to contact the call center (this was before online support was prevalent). At the end of the year, customers could decide whether to renew their subscription. If they had never called in with a problem, they might conclude they didn't get value from their investment. The most successful subscription services salespeople (say *that* three times fast!) were those who helped businesses find the right level of service for the next year—a higher level where it was needed, and a lower level if their service had previously been underutilized.

Some of you may be thinking, hey, they left money on the table for those customers who didn't use all of their services! The goal is to try to get the most business possible from the customer, right? This, readers, is short-term thinking: trying to maximize the amount of revenues this quarter or year. This type of thinking backfires when customers realize they have been overpaying for services they don't use and, worse, weren't told they could have switched to a subscription whose offerings were a better fit.

The long-term viewpoint dictates that we want our customers to have the *right* level of service, which may mean that they choose a lower level of service with us. But if it is the right level of service *for them*, they will ultimately be more satisfied. Customer satisfaction, when nurtured, can lead to long-term loyalty, which in turn can lead to increased positive word of mouth. That is what right-selling is all about.

JUST WHAT I NEEDED

You may find it necessary to craft differentiated experiences based on the life cycles and needs of your various customers. You can accomplish this very easily by asking customers a single question which helps you differentiate customers from each other based on their needs. The right question to ask may be simple to identify, or it may be determined through the more involved interpretation of data and analytics. However you decide to find the appropriate question to ask, this type of customized treatment strategy will go a long way toward helping you help your customers be successful, which, in turn, will bring them back for more.

Whether your customers are consumers or businesses, developing a solid understanding of them (who they are, what they want, and how they use what you offer or produce) makes all the difference in the sales and marketing process. How do your customers shop your business? What would make it easier to buy from you? Craft your own customer buying experience around the answers to those questions, and you will find an increase not only in sales but also in new customers as the word spreads that your company is outstanding when it comes to meeting customer needs.

Case Study
Teradata Builds Close Customer Relationships

Teradata Corporation is the world's largest company devoted solely to data warehousing and enterprise analytics. Since the company's founding in 1979, it has had a history of customer focus. In fact, while it was still a technology start-up, and before it had customers, Teradata asked prospects to help guide product development.

In 2009, Teradata asked Alan Chow to take on the role of chief customer officer (CCO), a newly created position that reports directly to Teradata President and CEO Mike Koehler. In this role, Chow is a member of the Teradata leadership team and is responsible for leveraging his extensive knowledge of Teradata's technology, products, and services to enhance customer satisfaction. As a customer advocate, Chow partners internally with the organization to ensure that its customer strategy reflects customer needs, and he helps customers who use Teradata products and services to become more successful.

Showing Value to Customers

One of Chow's main areas of focus is to ensure that Teradata customers receive the highest return on their investment (ROI) with Teradata, from *their* perspective. He wants customers to be able to see the value, track their own ROI, and understand how they can extend their use of business intelligence. Chow discussed the way Teradata helps customers build their own scorecard in this area as well as helps them closely track the value they're receiving from Teradata on a regular basis. He feels this is the key to ongoing success for customers in their use of data warehousing, as well as to the continuing relationship between Teradata and its customers.

The second most important area of focus for Chow is to help customers and prospects learn from one another. Rather than learning more about Teradata's technology road map, customers want to see case studies of how others are using Teradata's technology successfully, so they can improve their own use of it. According to Chow, as a result of these types of requests, "Our customers have become our second-most important asset besides our intellectual property."

Customers Take the Lead

Teradata customers play a front-and-center role with the organization. Since 1986, the PARTNERS Conference has been helping customers connect with each other, and it has become one of the most highly regarded events in the industry. Chow says that even in tough times, when customers may cut back on other expenditures, they always prioritize this event—and rightly so, since it is completely led by customers. The customer committee that oversees the conference solicits and selects more than 300 presentations to be given each year at the event (more than 700 papers are usually submitted). Customers present two-thirds of these papers, with no more than one-third given by Teradata and its business partners and suppliers. The conference is set up to provide customers with maximum networking time that allows them to mingle and swap stories with one another and build their networks. "This has been a very successful way of involving our customers," states Chow.

PARTNERS is part of a nonprofit organization, Partners User Group, run by Teradata customers. Along with the Steering Committee that sets up and manages the conference, there are three other customer-run committees. The Product Advisory Committee includes 15 customers who meet and review product enhancement requests from customers (which anyone can submit) for its base products. They prioritize the requests and meet with Teradata four times per year to present the suggestions. For each release cycle of the products, Teradata reserves a portion of its research and

(continued)

(*continued*)

development (R&D) resources specifically to implement the top priorities of its customers.

Another product advisory council for Teradata's analytics applications is organized in a similar fashion; there is also a service-focused team that provides input on how the data center operates its system. The latter is sponsored by Teradata's customer service organization. According to Chow, "We want to make sure [that] what we do with our service on a customer site is meeting our customers' needs." Chow also pointed out that these committee positions are highly coveted by customers, who have to be selected by their peers who sit on those committees in order to serve on them.

Customer Culture above All

Teradata uses all of these approaches to systematically receive input from customers, build relationships with them, and ingrain their feedback into Teradata products and the company overall. Chow feels that the reason Teradata is so successful, in spite of competing against companies with many more resources, is because its customer-focused culture is not just found in sales, service, or marketing; it's also integrated within Teradata's R&D organization. Teradata's Customer Greeting Center is housed within the heart of its R&D facility, rather than at corporate headquarters or in a marketing center. Teradata encourages R&D engineers and systems architects to take advantage of these visits by interacting personally with customers and prospects face-to-face; this directly exposes them to what customers are saying. Per Chow, "I firmly believe this is why Teradata engineers are able to out-innovate the competition in data warehousing."

Information taken from a personal interview with Alan Chow on January 14, 2011.

Chapter 3

COMMUNICATE WITH AND BECOME A FAN OF YOUR CUSTOMERS

W e ask our customers to buy our products, join our loyalty programs, even "Like" us on Facebook. We strive to inspire "raving fans." But are we fans of our customers? Fan-ship should be a two-way street. To get there, companies need to build relationships with their customers over time, doing little things on an ongoing basis to build trust and loyalty. It all starts with customer-focused communications. How, where, and how often you communicate with your existing customers can make a world of difference in this effort. The goal is to create conversational marketing that enhances the relationship.

Think about it: Can you get to know a new person you meet without having some kind of conversation? Whether it's in person, via e-mail, or on a Facebook wall, there has to be some type of interaction to move the relationship forward. Customer relationships are no different! In order to connect, marketers need to be willing to communicate the way their customers prefer, initiate a conversation, then keep it going—and just spend time getting to know them.

MARKETING THE WAY YOUR CUSTOMERS PREFER IT

Unfortunately, the communications that many brands send out don't always seem relevant to their existing customers. For example, a company might attempt to get a customer to "try a product" that has already been purchased, or it might promote new products and services that aren't the least bit interesting or relevant to the customer. It is important to use what we already know about our customers in order to communicate with them in a way that is most appropriate for them. When we approach our customers according to their preferences, they see that we're trying to relate to them on their level. Rather than forcing our company's way of doing things on our customers, we are seeking to help them achieve their own goals in the ways best suited to them.

There are several ways that we can begin to show our current customers that not only do we appreciate that they are fans of our brand but also we are actually striving to be *their* fans.

Speak Jargon-Free

Are your organization's marketing communications easy to read and interpret, or do your customers need a "code book" to decipher what you are saying? You have probably experienced the frustration of listening to people speak using their industry's lingo, perhaps in a doctor's office or when speaking to a lawyer. For example, customer service reps at a high-tech company might use "tech talk" when they answer technical questions posed by users. Or a services firm might use consulting buzzwords when selling their services to potential clients. Even a blogger might use "blog speak" to describe posts and plug-ins when they are sharing their passion for blogging with others who don't read blogs on a regular basis.

Keep in mind, your customers won't know or care about the latest buzzwords or corporate jargon. They want to hear what you have to say expressed in language they can understand. They want to be able to relate to what a company is offering to see if it fits their needs.

In Chapter 1, we looked at several ways to listen to your customers in order to learn how they feel about your products and services. Sales and marketing teams can use some of those methods to understand the actual words used by customers who are already talking about your company, your products, or your industry with their families, friends, colleagues, and social media connections. For example, do they talk about the load speeds of your "Web portal experience," or do they complain about how slow your Web site is? Do they lament about "opting out" of e-mails, or do they wonder how to stop getting so many messages from you? Spend time reading verbatim customer comments in surveys and online to learn not only their preferred terminology but also how your products and services fit into their lives or businesses. Talk to your sales and customer service teams to validate what you have learned and to unearth any nuances.

Once your teams get a handle on the language your customers use, you can begin to craft your communications *in their words* for all outgoing marketing, service, and online messaging from your Web site or social media sites.

Use Their Preferred Channel

Communicating with customers is most effective when we interact with them where they prefer to do so. For example, I have a friend who prefers to talk on the phone or communicate with me via e-mail. On the other hand, when I want to reach my teenagers, I text them on their cell phones; they rarely use their cell phones to talk, and they don't use e-mail. To have the best opportunity to be heard by your customers, your company needs to understand their preferred communication channels.

For example, if your company is reaching out to teens, you may find that they prefer YouTube instead of your company Web site. One of my teenagers was in the market for an Apple iPod—specifically, the iPod Touch. He had been saving up for one, but he wanted to learn more about it before taking the plunge. Here are the steps he took on his quest for knowledge:

1. *"I wanted to see what the iPod Touch was like, so I went to Apple's Web site."* He went to the iPod section from the toolbar at the top. From there, he saw what looked very promising: a video, "iPod Touch—A Guided Tour," which he clicked on to view. This is where the Apple Web site fell short. Instead of making the video easily accessible, my son was required to download Apple's QuickTime on his PC. He tried this but couldn't get it to work properly. At that point, he gave up on the Apple Web site.
2. Next stop: YouTube. Why? *"I know that a lot of people make videos of things they buy and how they work."* He quickly found a video tour

of the iPod Touch (it looked like it could have been put out by Apple) and spent the next 14 minutes glued to the computer screen. *"Wow, this is so cool! I really want one now, and I already know how to use it just by watching the video."*

3. His comment about how he intends to proceed next time: *"From now on, I am just going to go to YouTube first!"*

To recap: A potential teen buyer wanted to spend big bucks on new electronics, but he wasn't fully convinced about the product. He initially visited the company Web site but ran into problems trying to get the information he needed to make his purchase decision. So he went to his trusted source for information, YouTube, where he found exactly what he needed to make his decision.

Do you know how your customers prefer to learn about your products and services? Would they like to get an e-mail from you, keep up with you via social media, watch a video, or even receive information via snail-mail? How do you know which information channels *they* prefer to use? It's simple: Just ask them!

SOCIAL MEDIA FOR ENGAGEMENT AND CONVERSATION

If you discover your customers actively use social media, it may be a potential communication channel through which to reach out and interact with them. Social media tools can be especially effective at engaging in conversations and building relationships with customers—both consumers and businesses.

The way customers perceive your company online is part of their experience with your organization. According to a study by Cone Research, Americans using social media to interact with friends also want to engage with their favorite organizations and brands via that channel.[1] Additionally, 60 percent of active online consumers feel they have a *stronger connection with and are better served by* companies when they can interact via social media. The study goes on to state, "... Americans are eager to deepen their brand relationships through social media." Customers definitely view their interactions with an organization via social media as an integral part of their relationship with that brand. Therefore, this element of the experience needs just as much attention from your company as other parts of the marketing strategy.

Too many companies, however, want to become involved on social media sites without really thinking about or fully understanding why. Perhaps a company manager has read an article or heard about the latest social media technology and wants to start using it as soon as possible, without first identifying the goal for its use or the most effective way to achieve that goal. Indeed, there are many viable reasons for using social media to market a business, but companies that want to use these tools need to be very clear about their objectives *before* investing time and money in them.

One of the most powerful reasons to market with social media is to build and strengthen relationships with existing customers.

Connecting with Customers

While many organizations use social media as a way to raise awareness and increase online PR, the "sweet spot" is in connecting with your existing customers and empowering them to interact with you, as well as with others on behalf of your brand. According to the book *Groundswell*, companies can use social media to do the following:[2]

- Listen to the conversations customers are sharing in social media.
- Talk with (not *at*) customers.
- Energize customers to talk about the brand to their friends.
- Support customers.
- Embrace customers in an effort to co-create with them.

Companies can focus on some or all of these goals for using social media when interacting with customers; which goals they choose will depend on the company's desire and capability to engage in ongoing social media interactions, as well as on how their customers want to participate.

In addition, there are two main areas where companies can use social media tools especially well with existing customers: to strengthen relationships and to keep customers informed and involved.

Strengthening Relationships

Customers don't necessarily want a relationship with a company or organization; what they want is to have relationships with the *people* who work
for that company or organization. Social media tools allow customers
to get to know the individuals behind the scenes. They get to see "real
people" and experience their personalities.

For one nonprofit organization, the most popular part of its Web site
is the link to its Flickr photo stream. Its clients and donors love to see
the faces of the people behind the operations, and they seek them out
when given a chance to attend a face-to-face event, such as a fundraising
dinner. Friendships formed online are extended into the offline arena.

This is a prime example of how customers who have positive online
interactions with the people in an organization come to trust them, a
key factor in building and sustaining customer relationships.

Keeping Customers Informed and Involved

Where traditional media is good at keeping customers *informed*, social
media excels at getting customers *involved*. For example, when devastat-
ing wildfires broke out in San Diego in 2007, information was spotty and
difficult to obtain in a timely fashion. The San Diego Zoo used its blog to
provide updates on how the fire had impacted the park. It allowed zoo
members and other San Diegans to get a "look inside" to see how animals had been affected, thus keeping the community informed about
the safety of the animals and availability of the park. It also provided
opportunities to help support the zoo's efforts in caring for the wildlife
and a means for taking action.

In short, customers who are more involved and engaged tend to form
longer and stronger relationships with organizations.

A Different Mind-Set

Part of the concern that some companies have about engaging their
customers in online conversations is that they have not previously been
engaging in *any* conversations with customers—online or offline. In the
past, marketing and PR used one-way communication vehicles, such as
advertisements, press releases, and articles or white papers. In today's
business world, ongoing, two-way interactions with customers are

recognized as the way to build customer relationships. Social media enables this type of conversation.

Ideally, the social media channel should be treated as just one of many ways to reach out and forge lasting relationships with customers. The simple fact is, if your customers are interacting online, you need to be out there with them, talking to them and learning from them in their online spaces, wherever they may be found.

Keys to Engage Existing Customers with Social Media

Organizations that are successful in using social media with their customers employ the technology as a tool to support their business goals, rather than as a strategy unto itself. The following are some of the keys to successfully incorporating social media into your business strategy:

- *Listen to customers.* Don't just assume your existing customers want to engage in a certain way or with certain social media sites. Instead, directly ask your customers or clients which social media sites they use, and how they use them. Would they like to engage with your business on those sites? If not, why not? What might convince them to use social media to communicate with you?
- *Make a plan.* Don't just begin to blog or start using Facebook because everyone else is doing it. Your social media strategy needs to be as well thought-out as the rest of your marketing mix, perhaps even more so, because of its very public nature. Set goals, define guidelines for your internal team, test these ideas with customers, and ask for their feedback. In other words, treat social media as a powerful marketing tool, and use the same rigor as you would for direct mail, e-mail, or other marketing tools.
- *Use trial and error.* The adage, "If at first you don't succeed, try, try again" was never more true than in the age of social media. For example, a sports and social club encountered some difficultly in its initial attempts to interact via Facebook. The club's members were definitely engaging through this medium, and the company was looking for ways to get customers more involved on its Facebook page. An early attempt was to use the "Send someone a beer" Facebook application, thinking it would be a perfect fit for this group of active adults, who often gathered for drinks after sports events were

over. This approach failed, however. Instead, what proved to be a big hit was to have the club itself post photos of their sports events and happy hour gatherings on the club's Facebook page. Many of the members began to view the Facebook page and tagged themselves in the photos. This drove more interaction with the club's Facebook page as their curious friends wanted to see the photos that were alluded to in the Facebook newsfeed.

Not a Campaign, a Relationship

Companies that have well-established relationships with their customers will discover that social media is a great complement to their existing tools for interacting with and deepening those relationships. In contrast, companies that have been engaging only in one-way communication with their customers may have to do some work to encourage their customers to engage with them in these new formats. This will not be accomplished by treating social media as simply another channel for a stand-alone campaign. Social media should be used on an ongoing basis to continue to stay top-of-mind with customers, increase trust, and build relationships. Companies will find their customers are eager and ready to interact in this way as long as the conversation is relevant to *their* needs.

Case Study

Sanuk Loves Its Customers in Return

Long-Distance High Five

Southern California–based Sanuk Footwear is a company that has developed a cultlike following. Its slogan: "They're not shoes. (They're sandals)" and smiley-faced logo bring a beach-style feeling to everything it does, and its customers relate well to it.

Sanuk's Social Media Manager, Rachel Gross, started the company's first e-newsletter, which went out to more than 10,000 customers. It was not, however, a product-centric communication.

Gross described it as "a love letter to our customers," which focused on thanking them for patronizing the company and telling them how much they meant to Sanuk. The love letter began, "Let us start by giving you a long-distance high five!" Customers thought this was awesome, but that was no surprise. Gross understands her client base, inside and out, and she works to develop brand advocates from the loyal Sanuk customer base. According to Gross, "You have to love them as much as they love your brand."

Don't Promote Your Product

Sanuk receives a lot of love letters back from its customers. Sentiments such as "I love your product" or "This is all I wear" appear all over Facebook, Twitter, as well as in e-mails that customers send directly to the company. Gross says Sanuk knows its "regulars" on these social networks by name, and the staff focuses on making sure they feel special. Sanuk doesn't push its products on the company's Facebook fan page; instead, it shares surf videos and photos from the pro athletes it sponsors on the "Sanuk team." The company gets good engagement by asking its customers questions on the fan page wall. Gross feels that Sanuk's most loyal fans are the *last* ones to whom they want to market. "Once we engage their hearts and minds, we can continue to grow that relationship. It's not about pushing the products; it has to be about building relationships, getting to know them, and creating trust."

Sanuk's Facebook page doesn't have a direct link to the Sanuk.com Web site. Nevertheless, Google Analytics of the Sanuk Web site indicate that thousands of visitors a month still come to Sanuk.com from Facebook. Sanuk tracks conversion rates by looking at how many visits via Facebook result in a sale, which allows the company to calculate its return on using social media as an engagement tool. Sanuk also measures the growth and involvement of its loyal customers on its Facebook fan page. Gross sees a growing number of customers who stop by the fan page just to say hello, share photos of themselves in their Sanuks, and participate in the conversation with Sanuk and each other. Sanuk likes to

(continued)

(*continued*)

encourage a "We love Sanuk together" community feeling among its customers.

"Carpe DM"

This community effect has had an impact on Sanuk in several ways, most recently as an outpouring of community support for one of its own. A long-time advocate and wearer of Sanuk sandals had been attending Tennessee's Bonaroo music festival when he died tragically from heat exhaustion. Shortly afterward, Gross started receiving e-mail after e-mail about this person, whom she had never met, and they all said the same thing: this fan had shared his love for Sanuk with everyone. Many people had met him only through the Inforoo community (an online community about all things Bonaroo), but they said he had told them about Sanuk and had convinced them to buy the sandals. Several of the e-mails proposed that Bonaroo attendees should wear Sanuks in his honor.

In one of these e-mails the writer said he was looking forward to wearing his "Carpe DM" Sanuks to the Bonaroo festival in 2011 (a play on the fan's online screen name on Inforoo). Gross loved the idea and immediately approached company founder Jeff Kelley about renaming one of the sandals from the Fall 2010 lineup after this loyal customer. Kelley agreed, and they did—even including an "In Memory Of" line on the sandal's hangtag.[3] According to Gross, there was no reservation whatsoever from the company on running with her idea, and this made her feel incredibly empowered. Says Gross, "It was a little thing, but it meant so much to his community. People really loved him and tied him to Sanuk; he was the 'Sanuk guy.'"

Building Relationships

It really is all about the customer for Sanuk. Its sandals are uniquely made; in fact, they may be the only footwear that some people can wear comfortably. Sanuk receives e-mails all the time from folks with medical conditions, sensory issues, and so on, stating how much they appreciate what Sanuk has given them: the chance to wear a comfortable pair of shoes (sandals). This brings home Gross's final tip on how to love your customers: "It doesn't matter whether your customers are consumers or businesses, or whether your product is fun or boring. The most important thing you can do for your customers is to have empathy. Understand their pain points, and then tell them how you solve that uniquely for them. This helps your customers know that you really understand who they are and what they need."

Information taken from a personal interview with Rachel Gross on December 8, 2010.

START AN ONGOING DIALOGUE

Each customer touch point (whether in marketing, sales, or customer service) should be part of the proactive, ongoing conversation you start and carry on with your customer. Ideally, this dialogue will always pick up from where it left off last time (note: this requires that you *remember the customer*). Each instance of the conversation helps build a more complete picture of the customer's habits, preferences, needs, and desires. In addition, this ongoing dialogue will keep your company top-of-mind for product replacements, renewals, future purchases, or potential referrals.

"Are You Glad to Hear from Me?"

Some companies think only about communicating proactively with their current customers once a year. They might send a holiday card; certain customers might even receive a gift. Think about that: What message are you sending to a customer who only hears from you once a year? How do you feel when the annual holiday card is the only communication you receive from a business (other than bills) all year long? Customer relationships are like any other bond: They require ongoing care and feeding if they are to grow and be sustained long term.

Stay Top-of-Mind—Yet Relevant—with Customers

When my family first moved to our current city, we decided to purchase season passes to a few local attractions we thought we would likely visit more than once. Usually, buying an annual pass sounds like a great idea, but too often it is used only once or twice then languishes in a drawer for the rest of the year. Thus, when it comes time to renew, the question in a customer's mind will be whether the pass was worth the money.

Several months after purchasing a season pass to one of the local parks, we received a fun postcard reminding us to look in that drawer. It read, in part: "Your Season Passport. You remember, don't you? That come-as-you-are, anytime ticket to fun you bought a while back and have only used . . . once? Maybe twice?" Immediately, it got me thinking, Yeah, they're right; I think we *have* only been twice since we got it! I read on: "Go ahead. Dig through that drawer in your kitchen, or that purse you put away last year [they know me so well!], dust off that poor neglected Passport, and treat yourself, your family or your friends to a little fun in the sun at a place like no other."

This is a great example of marketing to customers in a way that is relevant to *them*, and it is a win-win for both customers *and* company. Customers who purchased this pass will benefit from the reminder and will probably come back to the park to check out new attractions or shows, at no additional expense. The park will benefit when these customers return, possibly bring friends, and, hopefully, purchase something while there (such as food, drinks, or gifts). And the biggest benefit will come at renewal time. This park started the renewal process early for us (about three months before expiration) and urged us to get good use from the season pass.

This is the magic moment for renewals: When customers look back at the cost of an annual subscription (whether for a season pass, a 12-month service contract, a Web subscription, etc.), they will consider whether they received enough value from it to renew. Often, companies forget to remind their customers of the value they have received from their subscription in the past year.

How do you remind your customers about the value your company, product, or service provides? If you have annual renewals, remember to remain visible to your customers by actively communicating the benefits that come from their subscription with you. This will help them realize that the relationship with you has been valuable to them. If your customers are businesses, sending a quarterly or annual report card detailing services delivered can be helpful in justifying value. Even if you don't have annual contracts, staying in touch with your existing customers will keep you in the forefront of their minds when they need your products or services in the future.

Here are more tips for staying in touch with existing customers:

- *Understand your customers' preferences,* as discussed earlier in this chapter. How do they want you to communicate with them? E-mail? Postcard? Phone? Facebook? Utilize their preferred methods of interacting with you, and keep in mind that this will vary from one customer to another.

- *Recognize where your customers are in the life cycle of doing business with your company.* Have they been customers for a long time? Are they within the first 30 days of doing business with you? Have they just referred new customers to you? Adjust your communications accordingly to acknowledge the position of the customers in their life cycle with your company, as well as the level of business they are doing with you.

- *Be relevant.* Most customers want to know you see them as more than just a name on a mailing list, so appeal to them in a way that relates to their experience and customary product or service preferences.

- *Intersperse up-sell and cross-sell communications with interesting, valuable information or "just because" communications.* These could include news items or industry statistics, birthday greetings, or customer stories. Give customers something of value—and not just when you want their business. (More on this in the next chapter.)

- *Initiate a quarterly "How are things going?" contact.* Connect regularly with customers to see how things are going and check on their satisfaction levels. This is a good way to let existing customers know you are thinking about them; conversely, it will prompt them to think more about *you.* It will also allow you to hear about and address any concerns raised during this contact—as long as you ask, of course!

Case Study
FreshBooks Becomes a Fan of Its Customers

One of the best ways to get to know your customers is to spend time with them, face-to-face. This method of doing business is a hallmark of a "Customers Rock!" company and is usually supplemented with other types of customer conversation that take place over traditional as well as social media channels. For Toronto, Canada–based invoicing company FreshBooks, this is not an unusual way to do business; rather, it is business as usual!

Unique Customer Outreach

Though FreshBooks provides online invoicing and time tracking for service businesses, it firmly believes there is no substitute for meeting customers face-to-face. CEO Mike McDerment likes to tell a story about one of the firm's most unique and effective customer outreach campaigns. McDerment was attending two conferences in the United States, along with Head of Magic at FreshBooks, Saul Colt, and a few other folks from the company. The final stop for the group was the South by Southwest Interactive Conference in Austin, Texas. Since they were coming from Toronto, clearly the easiest and fastest way to get there would have been to fly. That was not, however, the route this team followed. They decided instead to take a completely different approach: They rented an RV so they could have the opportunity to meet and dine with customers along the way. Calling it the "RoadBurn" tour, they also started a RoadBurn blog[4] to chronicle the trip. (Several customers even used the blog to request the group stop in their towns.)

The FreshBooks team described the intent of the road trip as follows: "The FreshBooks RoadBurn may seem like a stunt or a marketing ploy, but in reality, it is pretty much what FreshBooks is all about: listening to its beautiful customer base and getting to know them on a level that other companies wouldn't make the effort to do." By the end of their trip, the FreshBooks team had eaten breakfast, lunch, and dinner with more than 100 customers during a period of 4 days.

This trip was *not* a product road show; rather, it was a *listening tour*. McDerment and his team didn't drive the mealtime conversations. They merely asked a few simple questions to get customers talking, such as, "Hey, how are you? What do you do?" Rather than peppering them with questions, they encouraged the customers to network among themselves. By the end of the meals, many of these customers were swapping business cards and planning to do business with each other. According to McDerment, the result was "almost a mini-ecosystem!"

Listening in on this type of environment provided fresh (get it?) customer insights about how customers were using the organization's products—and gave the RoadBurn team information they could never have attained simply by conducting a survey.

Getting to Know You

This road trip was really nothing new for FreshBooks. The firm had been holding these "customer meals" for about four years prior to starting RoadBurn, and they continue to do so. McDerment and Colt explain that each time one of them travels to a city, he gets a list of FreshBooks customers in that city. He then invites these clients to dinner to hear what is going on with their business and to introduce them to other local FreshBooks customers. As you can imagine, this is very effective for building customer relationships and for promoting invaluable word of mouth. Recently, they took 45 customers bowling in New York, and according to Colt, it was almost twice as enjoyable as dinner because everyone got to move around and really talk to one another. McDerment declares, "We are conscious that there is always someone on the other end of the computer screen who is using our products. We keep asking ourselves, how can we get closer to our customers? Also, we want to help our customers focus on and do what they love; a huge part of that is enabled by finding more business. These events help them build a network, and we help facilitate that."

(continued)

(*continued*)

Caring—A Core Value

Customer care is embedded in the corporate culture at FreshBooks; it's in their company DNA. McDerment supports this in a number of ways. One, he hires for fit, a process he describes as seeking out employees who feel good about helping other people. Two, he gives employees the space they need to do what is necessary for the customer. Members of the customer support team (who all have the title of Support Rockstar) have done things in the past such as sending a gaming headset to an existing customer who had recently become disabled, thereby allowing the customer to more effectively use a computer. In another instance, a Support Rockstar sent out a gift certificate to a customer who was a cancer patient. McDerment doesn't always know about these initiatives, and that's okay with him. Colt pointed out that FreshBooks employees send out these types of items to cheer people up or to make their lives easier, not to promote the company. They aren't distributing items emblazoned with the company logo; rather, they're sending gifts that "are intended to help make that person's life better." Colt himself once sent out a box of cookies that were available only locally to a customer who had just moved to Fiji and had commented on Twitter how much he missed his favorite local foods.

In addition, everyone at FreshBooks does a rotation in customer support—an experience that gives all team members the opportunity to hear from customers directly and to understand their pain points. In fact, a new employee can expect to spend the first four to six weeks on the support desk before they start their own jobs, regardless of what type of role that may be. McDerment explains, "It is the best way to get to learn about our customers and our products." He also shared that he just took a "support holiday" himself. During that time, he didn't attend any executive meetings; instead, he concentrated on customer service, answering phones and replying to e-mails. He described how this helps him stay in touch with FreshBooks' customers and reinforce the energy around the company's customer service culture.

McDerment says one of the core values of FreshBooks is caring. As CEO, he is always taking care of employees, making sure they have what they need for their jobs and looking out for their happiness and health. According to McDerment, the formula for success is as follows:

Take care
of staff   →   Staff takes care
of customers   →   Customers take
care of referrals

Results

The formula is one that has worked well for FreshBooks. According to its customer satisfaction surveys, the company typically has a customer referral rate of 98 to 99 percent. As McDerment states, "There is really nothing better. Happy customers are a great pool of positive word of mouth."

Information taken from personal interviews with Mike McDerment and Saul Colt on January 14, 2011.

Chapter 4

CAPTURE, THEN REWARD, THEIR BUSINESS

Many companies spend a lot of time and money trying to attract new customers to their product or service. They spend a good portion of their marketing budgets on mass approaches such as advertising and direct mail. While those media have their place in *finding* new prospects, frequently they are not as helpful in *keeping* a company's most valuable asset: their existing customer base.

What does the content of your marketing communications say about how much your company values its *current* customers? Interactions with existing customers tend to fall into one of the following categories: a bill, an up-sell offer, a cross-sell attempt, or a renewal offer. There may be some customer value in these actions, but they tend to benefit the company more than the customer. In fact, customers who answered a survey on their feelings about regular company communications expressed frustration with what they do receive. Nearly 54 percent of existing customers stated that if companies kept sending what they, the customers, perceived as spam and irrelevant messages, they would disconnect from those communications altogether.[1]

Customers want to know that you value their business. They want to know that *you know* how long they have been with you, and they want to feel appreciated. Showing customers that you do indeed care about them is one of the most effective ways to capture their business for the long term. A well-planned communication strategy that balances customer appreciation notes, informational tidbits, and a sprinkling of relevant sales messages will result in stronger customer relationships than heavy marketing campaigns could hope to achieve. And especially in a tough economy, creating content your current customers care about can mean the difference between achieving your sales and retention goals and failing to do so.

SEND MORE THAN JUST BILLS

Reflect back on the last three communications you received from a company with which you do business. What were they? Most likely, they were marketing pieces that the company deemed important to send, such as an up-sell, a sales offer, or, inevitably, a bill or an invoice. Now think about what you might have *preferred* to receive from that company: news that's important to you, a thank-you note, acknowledgment of your longevity as a customer, or perhaps an announcement of a special deal on an upcoming promotion for a product that is complementary to one you already own.

The Messages Your Marketing Communications Send

Every "touch" from every department in your organization is marketing, whether or not the communicator has the official title of "marketer." Each customer interaction that takes place, whether by phone, e-mail, direct mail, social media, or the Web, leaves an impression about your brand. So ask yourself: Are your marketing communications self-serving, or do they serve customer needs?

Not long ago, I came across this lament from a prominent blogger about the communications he received from an electronics retailer:

My reward for spending around $10,000.00 since joining the [loyalty] program . . . and the most recent offer following the holiday season? A Credit Card Offer!! Man, do I feel special. This is a campaign, nothing more. Marketing 1.0. . . . Monetize your list, not build better relationships with your "special" customers.

Consider what messages the following communications convey to your customers about *your* company. How would they feel after receiving each of these types of messages?

Bills and Invoices

No organization can avoid sending bills and invoices to customers; after all, they are a necessary part of doing business. But if these are the *only* communications your customers receive from your company, chances are they feel you are interested in them only for the money you can make from them. Is that really the message you want to send?

Newsletters

Company or product newsletters, sent either by direct mail or e-mail, can go a long way toward keeping your company top-of-mind with your customers—but only if these publications are interesting and relevant. So consider carefully the kinds of messages you are sending in them.

One company I'm familiar with, which offers several different product lines, produced a separate newsletter for each of them. That meant if a customer owned more than one product from that company (obviously, an ideal situation from its point of view), that customer would receive multiple newsletters. Preferably, customers would receive only one comprehensive yet "customized" newsletter that incorporated all of the company's product announcements and information in one easily accessible piece.

Are your communications formatted for your customers' convenience or for yours?

New Product Announcements

Businesses, of course, want to share new product information with their customers. The question is, do their customers always want to hear it? If so, what do they want to hear about, specifically?

Product and service information is most helpful to customers when it is relevant to their interests and complementary to existing products or services they already buy from you. Be careful not to send product promotions to customers who already own that product. This essentially announces to your customers that you have no idea how or why they do business with you. Similarly, beware of sending "Welcome to our company!" letters to all new customers who purchase from you; you may end up sending it to some who already use your products and services!

E-Mail

In this day and age of concerns about information privacy, we all know that permission-based e-mails are critical. However, content and relevance of these e-mails are also important. If the e-mail's subject and body aren't consistent with your relationship with customers, you will cause them to question their trust in you, which may prompt them to unsubscribe. I recently saw an example in which a customer hadn't heard from a particular company for months (actually he couldn't recall when he'd last heard from them, if at all). On this particular day, the previously silent company sent this customer an e-mail message that looked more like a grouping of advertisements for partners than a valuable communication. The company appeared to regard its customers more as a list to be mined or sold rather than as relationships to be nurtured. This highlights the fact that e-mail frequency, relevancy, and content are all essential to building those relationships in a positive, constructive way.

Phone Calls

Telephone communications with customers will be closely scrutinized and possibly dismissed quickly, since they interrupt a customer's already busy schedule. What kinds of calls are you making to your current customers, if any? For example, frequently calling to "tell you about a new service we think you will like" is annoying, at best. On the other hand, calling to let customers know you appreciate their business, then asking for feedback on a recent interaction with your company is more likely to be received openly and positively. Be careful, though: Customers will be quick to notice if you "slip in" promotions to these calls. I remember receiving a call from my insurance agent wishing me a happy birthday. Nice, I thought—until he slipped in a soft-sell for the company's long-term care insurance. This approach might have made sense to him, but it felt inappropriate to me. In contrast, I received a call from a realtor, congratulating my family on our two-year anniversary in our house. Notably, he was the realtor who had represented the *seller*, not the buyer (us), yet he continues to maintain contact with us on a regular basis, just to say hello and cement the relationship. Suffice it to say, I know who we will call when we are ready to move into another house.

Social Media

These days, many of your existing customers will expect you to use social media channels as a way to interact with them directly. When you use social media to communicate with your customers, what does it say about your company? If you post completely self-serving information (i.e., only sharing items about your company, brand, or products), customers will lose interest, quickly. But when you send communications that provide something useful to customers, or that allow them to get to know the people behind the company name, you will begin to strengthen your customer relationships.

Anyone who follows the CEO of online retailer Zappos on Twitter (found on http://twitter.com/zappos) knows what I mean. On his Twitter feed, they will find fun and sometimes-funky information about what's happening at Zappos, in addition to the occasional product announcement and contest. Not only is this engaging, customers also feel they are getting a behind-the-scenes glimpse at Zappos and the personalities of its employees—notably, its leader.

Package Inserts

When you send out a customer order, what goes in the box along with the product? Most likely, a receipt or an invoice. One simple way to capture a customer's attention is to also enclose a simple thank-you note. The best one I received was from a small Internet-based company called The Busy Bunny (http://busybunny.com). In the box with my order was a handwritten note that read "Thank you for your business," on a Busy Bunny–branded notepad (a freebie). Totally unexpected, it brought a smile to my face—and I feel good about that company every time I use the notepad!

Persist in Offering Value

Offering something of value to your customers, as illustrated in the communications examples described above, and at the right frequency for those customers, is important to furthering relationships with them. If you fail to provide value, or if communications are too frequent, they may continue to do business with you for a while. However, chances are the relationship will ultimately be short-lived.

As I've said before, to be relevant to your customers you need to listen to and get to know them. Then, you can use that customer understanding plus any history of past purchases, behaviors, and preferences to offer communications that show (1) you *really* know your customers and (2) you are using that knowledge to send information that is relevant to them.

Maintaining this laser-focus on current customers allows companies to keep buyers engaged in the communication, whether or not they've purchased something recently. This is one of the keys to capturing and retaining a customer's ongoing business.

WHY DO ONLY NEW CUSTOMERS GET THE BEST DEALS?

I have been a customer of a particular company for over 20 years (it is the only provider in my area). Frequently, I receive offers that look interesting at first glance, but on perusing the fine print, I often discover that these offers are for "new customers only." Other mailings I receive misspell my name or address me as "Dear Friend." I have to wonder: Is this company really my friend?

A quick Google search on the phrase "new customers only" turns up offers from companies ranging from consumer utilities to financial services firms to dairies. From a company perspective, these "trial offers" no doubt seem like a great way to attract new visitors or customers.

But how might a company's long-time, loyal customers feel about such promotions? A few words come to mind: angry, cheated, not valued, and unappreciated. They may feel—justifiably so—that the company cares more about attracting new customers than keeping their loyal ones. Very likely, it also sends the message to existing customers that they have to go to a competitor to get the best deal.

Is it worthwhile for organizations to be so intent on capturing new customers through these offers that they risk disappointing existing customers, possibly to the point of losing them? It might be better to spend some of that budget to keep existing customers happy, grow them into more frequent or active customers, and let *them* spread the word.

Encouraging customer word of mouth through formal or informal referral programs can be more effective than any number of "new customer deals." You can accomplish this by giving existing customers the right incentives—those that are meaningful to them—for sharing their brand experiences with others in their network.

Referrals Are Valuable

Customers are more likely to trust the anecdotes about companies shared by their peers and others they perceive to be similar to themselves than they are marketing communications from brands. Not all of your customers are going to be A-list bloggers who can influence the masses, but most of your customers do know others who, like them, could benefit in some way from what your company has to offer. Again, this is a more cost-effective way to bring in new prospects. In fact, according to a study titled "Referral Programs and Customer Value," referred customers are 16 percent more valuable than new customers that were not referred; they are also more likely to stay.[2]

Here are three tips that will make it easier for your customers to share the good news with others:

1. *Ask them.* You can't assume that customers will run out and shout from the rooftops about the great experience they just had with your company. You may have to give some guidance and encouragement to motivate customers to share with their peers what it was like to deal with your company. And it all starts by asking them for a referral. The best time to do this is within the first few weeks after customers have received delivery of a product or service, when they are most likely to experience maximum satisfaction, and remember it.

   As part of the request, be sure to offer guidance to customers for thinking about who they might know that would benefit the most from your services. For example, if the customer is a member or leader of a professional or community association, you might suggest sharing with a peer or two at the next chapter meeting. Or if the customer actively uses social media, you could encourage that person to reach out to two or three social media contacts to let them know about your business. By putting forward these suggestions, you help customers determine their plan of action, which will remind them of your request the next time they interact with their group.

2. *Offer refer-a-friend deals.* Referrals are much more powerful than new customer deals; when a customer recommends your business to friends or acquaintances, those friends are more likely to take that recommendation than respond to a company's "new customer deal."

When creating referral incentives, be sure they provide benefits to both the current customer making the referral and the new customer. Customers, obviously, will need to know about the program to participate, and the ongoing marketing dialogue discussed previously can help promote both the program and its benefits. Customers who use social media could also promote the program via social network updates, stating that they just referred a friend or colleague and got a reward. Don't forget to track the referral benefits closely to ensure that they provide the best returns, as well as the desired customer actions.

3. *Offer incentives for using social media.* Certain social media tools lend themselves well to customer ratings and reviews, and these can lead to customer trials. While these are not necessarily as powerful as one-to-one referrals, they may be more "user-friendly" for those customers who feel uncomfortable directly approaching a friend or colleague to make a company or product recommendation. In this regard, some loyalty programs give extra points to customers who post a rating or review on a social media site, such as Yelp! or TripAdvisor. Just be sure *never* to require customers to post positive reviews; falsely positive reviews are easy to spot by savvy prospects. And don't be afraid of possibly receiving negative comments! If you have built strong relationships with your existing customers, they will come to your rescue and help refute the claims. Furthermore, customer problems and complaints posted online give you the opportunity to publicly address those concerns, and that could be just the catalyst for a now-satisfied customer to share the good news about your company with others.

Win-Win

Customer referrals have positive effects on both company and customer. The more your company can prioritize growing its bottom line through its existing customers, either by expanding business with them or through referrals, the more effective you can be allocating your marketing budget. The more a customer feels rewarded for doing business with you, either by having their needs met or by bringing in new customers, the more passionate they will be about your brand. Good feelings all around!

THANK YOU FOR BEING A CUSTOMER—I MEAN IT!

Customers are the most valuable asset your company has; after all, without them you wouldn't be in business. With that in mind, ask yourself when is the last time you thanked a customer? I don't mean the obligatory "Thank you for your business" spoken at the end of a transaction or written on the bottom of an invoice or receipt. I am talking about genuine, heartfelt expressions of appreciation. This sounds simple, yet it is amazing how many companies don't do this, or don't do it well.

How do I thank thee? Let us count the ways.

Personal Thanks

Writing thank-you notes is becoming less and less common. These days, it is almost always a surprise—and a pleasant one—when someone sends a sincere and personal thank-you note. So one obvious way to differentiate yourself and your business from your competition is by sending customers handwritten thank-you notes. There are only a handful of times I have received a handwritten note from a business, and I can remember them all. Among the standouts: Salon Radius (a hair salon profiled in Chapter 13) following my first visit; Coldwater Creek, a clothing retailer, after buying a large number of items in one of their mall stores; and online retailer The Busy Bunny, mentioned earlier in this chapter.

A handwritten thank-you note is one of the best ways to recognize customers. Make it easy to write thank-you notes between appointments or sales calls by keeping a stack of note cards and envelopes handy, with postage already on them. Another way to make it easy is to have mailing labels automatically printed out with a customer receipt. Sales reps, retailers, or customer service personnel can write them during off-peak hours. One company I know decided to send out one thank-you note to a different customer every day; by the end of the year, it had reached more than 300 customers with personal notes of appreciation!

It takes only a few minutes to write each short note, but doing so can guarantee you customers for life.

One final tip here: Be sure to address your customers by name, and make the content sincere and personal. I assure you, this will be time well-spent.

Social Media Thanks

Sometimes it works best to thank customers where they interact most frequently. Social media is ideal for this, providing a quick, public method to show appreciation to customers who spend time in these channels. Here is an example. I teach a class called "Marketing via New Media" at the University of California–San Diego. After class one night, one of my students, who worked for a company that sells flowers, asked me what to do about a newly found raving fan. I suggested that she and her company reach out to that fan and personally thank that customer. My student did just that—with great results.

Here's how it played out: The new fan was so pleased with the bouquet sent by her husband from my student's company that she wrote a note about it on Twitter. The company was listening for customer input via social media and saw the fan's Tweet. Via its own Twitter handle, a customer rep responded: "So glad you liked your Valentine's Day sunshine!!!" The flower company then proceeded to thank her for her Tweet by sending a surprise bouquet!

This was indeed a surprise to the fan, who then was inspired to write about her experience via her own blog. In it, she shared the story of receiving the original bouquet sent by her husband, the great customer service from the company (a rep had called her husband to make sure the delivery went well), and, finally, the surprise bouquet that arrived a few days later.

As a result of the post and Tweets from this highly satisfied customer, my student's flower company gained at least two new customers, as well as new followers on Twitter. Clearly, it struck a chord with consumers who want to do business with a company that cares about people. It also did an effective job listening and responding to customer conversations via both social media and offline (i.e., sending the bouquet).

Are your customers using social media channels to talk about how much they love your product or brand and to share their positive experiences with you? Remember, if you are listening to customers (as discussed in Chapter 1), you will be able to participate in these conversations. Thank them for their business on the social media channel where they mentioned your company. For example, if you run a restaurant, you might thank them for coming ("Nice to see you last night; hope you enjoyed your meal!"), thank them for their consistent patronage ("Thanks for being a loyal fan!"), or thank them for their kind words ("Thanks for recommending us to your friends. You rock!"). Not only will your customers be pleased that you "tuned in," others will also see your thank-you notes to customers and be attracted to your business.

Pure Thanks

I read an example of a meaningful interaction between a patron and a pizza restaurant. In response to filling out the (optional) customer contact card, this customer received an e-mail from the store manager thanking her for her business. She sent back a quick reply, stating that she loved the pizza; she then received another message—this time from a *company VP* thanking her for her feedback.

Here's the kicker: Nowhere in these e-mail messages did any selling take place. No promotions or offers were presented. There was simply an expression of customer appreciation and an implied invitation to keep the lines of communication open. As a result of initiating a conversation with this customer by sending e-mails of appreciation, this pizza restaurant most likely will be rewarded with a long relationship with her.

Just Do It

Why do these experiences make such an impact? The simple fact is that very few businesses take the time to thank their customers. When they do, customers see them as exceeding expectations, and this stands out and is long remembered.

Have you thanked a customer lately? The best companies don't do this randomly; they make thanking and interacting with customers a regular part of doing business. It is integrated into their marketing plans. It is taught in their customer service training sessions. It is modeled by managers who thank employees. It becomes part of a company's culture.

So take a minute, right now, to let two or three of your best customers know you appreciate them, *without* trying to up-sell or cross-sell them. Write a thank-you note, call them, or send them a message via their favorite social network. Let them know they are important to you!

MAKE CUSTOMERS FEEL VALUED

Not all customers want to be rewarded in the same way. Even though they may look the same in your customer database based on demographics and psychographics, what is important to one customer may not be of any interest to the next despite other similarities they may share. Understanding your customers and their needs is the critical first step in rewarding them appropriately. This is how to begin to unlock their power to become advocates for your business.

Speak Their Language

In a popular book called *The 5 Love Languages*,[3] written by marriage and family life expert Dr. Gary Chapman, you can read about the five different ways people in relationships say "I love you." They are as follows:

1. Words of Affirmation
2. Quality Time
3. Receiving Gifts
4. Acts of Service
5. Physical Touch

Applying some of the principles from this book, we can also learn something about how customers want to be "loved." Understanding what is important to your customers is vital to making them feel valued by your organization.

Words of Affirmation

This takes the form of appreciation and recognition expressed in a written or verbal fashion. For the type of customer who responds to this "love language," it is important to hear phrases such as "You are valuable to us," "You are one of our best customers," or "We really appreciate your business." As long as these words are conveyed *sincerely*, and not offered up to just anyone, they will speak volumes to these customers.

Quality Time

This "love language" requires spending meaningful time building a relationship, and for some customers this is extremely important. Other customers may not really care about developing a relationship with your organization, but for those who do, the conversation you carry on with them is important. These are the customers who appreciate blogs and other social media that allow them to speak their mind to a company. They also want to know that the organization will take the time to answer back. This generates a dialogue and deepens customer loyalty.

Receiving Gifts

Many organizations feel the need to send gifts to their best customers. Is this effective? It depends. If the gift is relevant and ties into the existing relationship, then it could be worthwhile. The gift does not necessarily have to be monetary to be effective for these customers. Traditional loyalty programs cater to this type of thinking. For those customers who value gifts, speaking this "love language" will help cement the relationship. It will not, however, work with every customer.

Acts of Service

The language of service is spoken when brands do something for the customer, and it is ideal for clients who appreciate outstanding treatment more than anything else. Some people simply don't care about earning rewards points; they just want quality customer service.

During interactions, the service "love language" can also be spoken by remembering things for and about customers. Does your company remember the account code I just typed in? Does it remember me from the last time I visited your store? Acts of service are valuable to most customers, but it is a loyalty key for those who long for this type of recognition.

Physical Touch

This last "love language" is a bit trickier to achieve in customer relationships! But for the purpose of this discussion, I equate it to "face time." For some customers, e-mail, phone, voicemail, and Twitter are ideal ways to update them, whereas other customers won't "seal the deal" until they have had face-to-face contact with someone at your company. They tend to think, "If you really care about me, then spend the time to come and meet me." This is especially relevant for B2B organizations, and it can be equally important to consumers. For example, some consumers prefer to stand in the grocery store checkout line staffed by a "live" cashier versus dealing with an automated self-service machine.

How well do you speak your customer's "love language"? Are you flexible enough to speak one way to one customer and another way to a different customer? Does your organization track the preferences of its best customers? Have you planned the customer experience well enough to take action on these preferences? Ask your managers these key questions during your staff meetings, and then make a plan based on their responses. For more on planning the customer experience, see Chapter 5.

Loyalty Programs That Work

Loyalty programs started out as a great idea: to reward customers for being frequent visitors and purchasers, with the goal of prompting them to do more shopping with the companies to which they were loyal. Today, if I look in my wallet, I will find a plethora of loyalty membership cards promising the opportunity to get more for less nearly everywhere I go. There is the grocery store (of course; who would shop without one of these cards and pay full price?), the office supply store, the shoe store, the hairdresser, the coffee house, the pet supply store. Too many to count.

A study conducted by the CMO (Chief Marketing Officer) Council found that 50 percent of marketing executives said their number one challenge was acquiring and retaining motivated and engaged customers.[4] Many companies believe that launching a customer loyalty or rewards program is an easy way to drive users to increase the amount of business they do with them. However, according to the same study, customer feedback on many loyalty programs indicated that they weren't always satisfied with these programs. They cited objections to certain requirements inherent in these types of programs, such as stringent redemption conditions; they also noted that many programs offered rewards that were not of value to them.

A customer loyalty program can have a very positive impact on customers and their attitude toward a company that executes the program well. Therefore, these kinds of programs need to be managed with as much care as the rest of your branding and marketing strategies. They work most effectively when they are relevant, drive a customer to action that furthers the relationship, and serve as a means of encouraging ongoing dialogue with the customer. Successful programs are those designed with the customer's needs in mind, rather than as thinly veiled ploys to access customer information for the company's benefit. A well-executed program will not only collect relevant customer information, it will promote the type of relationship where customers *willingly* give the type of information about themselves, which then becomes a competitive advantage for the business. In sum, the best loyalty programs are not really programs as much as they are a way of doing business for a company.

Tips for Valuing Customers

Making customers feel valued goes a long way toward strengthening your organization's customer base. The following are some tips for organizations that want to grow their business by capturing, then rewarding, their current customers:

- Understand who your best customers are and what they need. Make sure every company contact, including marketing and advertising, expands the relationship with these "bread-and-butter" customers.
- Explore what you can do to make it easier for your best customers to do business with you.
- Take what you learn from your best customers and apply it to your other existing customers, and even to your prospects. You may find that some of them "grow up" to be your new best customers.

- Consider how existing customers view introductory offers to new customers. Enlist their help by offering them something in return for bringing you new customers.

At the end of the day, it's all about people. Customers are no different from anyone else; they want to be noticed and treated with respect. If I am your customer, I want you to show me that you have learned something, *anything*, from my past interactions with you. And if you do know something about me, use it appropriately to make it more convenient for me to buy from you. Make me feel that I matter to you (if I do). If I don't matter to you, don't try and make it look as if I do; the insincerity will be obvious. Send me personal communications that I would want to receive; by doing so, you will most likely stand out from your competitors.

This kind of thinking helps feed a strong customer strategy, which will extend relationships to the point at which customers become advocates for your company and its products or services. If you are involved in your customer community and are using their lingo and way of thinking, finding and empowering customer advocates will be a natural outcome of the way you do business.

Case Study
Marriott Rewards Its Customers

Marriott International is a leading hotel company with more than 3,500 lodging properties located in 70 countries; under its umbrella are such brands as Marriott Hotels & Resorts and The Ritz-Carlton Hotels. Started by J. W. Marriott, Sr., Marriott International has a long-standing tradition of "doing whatever it takes to take care of the customer." It executes this tradition through a keen focus on its employees (called "associates") by directing them to "Take care of your employees, and they'll take care of your customers." This deeply held belief, started by Mr. Marriott Sr., remains the keystone of the company's culture.

(continued)

(*continued*)

With a strong corporate culture that is committed to the care of its associates and customers, a loyalty program proved to be a good fit for Marriott. Its first frequent-guest program, started in 1983, has grown into Marriott Rewards, a program that is 35 million members strong. Customer communications occur in a variety of ways, including via direct mail, e-mail, the company Web site (these are the most popular pages on Marrriott.com), and an online community, in addition to direct customer contact at Marriott properties.

Marriott's Senior Director of Customer Relationship Marketing, Michelle Lapierre, explains that Marriott Rewards is more than just a loyalty program; it is really a way to take care of customers. Lapierre shared stories with me that showcased the variety of customer "life moments" that have come about because of the program. For example, one woman used her Rewards Points to stay near a hospital where her spouse was receiving medical treatment. A family that had lost power during a local emergency was able to use their points to stay, safe and sound, at a Marriott hotel. A frequent guest was given the surprise honor of cutting the ribbon to a new gym at the Marriott hotel where he often stayed (he had been looking forward to using the gym for months while it was under construction). According to Lapierre, these types of moments come naturally for Marriott and its guests because Marriott associates have a "heartfelt desire to make people happy."

They are also indicative of the affection between Marriott and its guests, apparent in the Marriott Rewards member online community, Marriott Insiders. The company sees its loyalty program as one giant brand advocacy group. Associates talk regularly to members about which benefits they prefer, and members readily share what would make their experience better. According to Lapierre, research shows that people have an expectation of being recognized at the places they go regularly. With so many opportunities for Marriott to interact with its customers around the world, the company uses its robust Customer Relationship Management (CRM) system to deliver relevant information on its members to those touch points, in order to help carry on a more personal conversation.

For example, Platinum members receive a gift when they check in to a Marriott property. And in order to generate better interaction and provide a more human touch, a card is presented to those members when they arrive at reception, asking them to check-off what they prefer as their gift. Platinum members have shared that Marriott, by recognizing them and their status, makes them feel special. Another meaningful, human interaction has taken place, adding an additional positive element to the Marriott Rewards customer experience and furthering the customer relationship between company and members.

Information taken from a personal interview with Michelle Lapierre on December 10, 2010.

R
O—ORCHESTRATE THE CUSTOMER EXPERIENCE
C
K

Taking the customer's perspective.

Customers don't buy a product or service in a vacuum; they buy it as part of an experience. In a tough economy, buyers hold on to their money more tightly, and for longer, as they make difficult choices about if, where, and when to spend it. When customers have a great experience with your company, it significantly increases the chances that they will come back to spend more of their time and money at your place of business, and that they will tell their friends, family, and colleagues about their positive interactions with you.

Every transaction and interaction your customer has with your organization has a "golden moment." If the interaction is positive, it unleashes the hidden power of your customer. If the interaction is negative, the golden moment is tarnished, and the hidden power of your customer is diminished. Sadly, it can take only one bad experience to ruin all the other positive experiences a customer has had with an organization. For this reason, the customer experience cannot be left to chance. "Customers Rock!" companies create a strategy for ensuring a consistent, enjoyable customer experience across the entire customer life cycle.

Chapter 5

PLAN THE EXPERIENCE

C ustomers today are more empowered than ever before. They have more choices in the marketplace. They are better informed thanks to the Internet and the research they can do easily before making buying decisions. They are collaborating in many new ways—both with each other and with organizations.

They also have higher expectations than ever before. No longer are they willing to settle for mediocre customer experiences. Every touch point a business or consumer has with a brand or organization leaves an impression of that brand and its products and services. That impression is affected by subsequent interactions with that organization, as well as by interactions at other organizations. For example, although I may be an executive for a large high-tech company, my customer experience expectations are created not just through my professional business dealings but also through my experiences as a consumer.

To their detriment, few companies are focused on how their customers experience doing business with them. But they should be; otherwise, they may find out the hard way after they have made a big mistake—and multiple blogs and YouTube videos pick it up and bring widespread attention to it. A study by Forrester Research, an independent technology and market research company, shows there is a high correlation between customer experience and three key metrics of customer loyalty:

1. Willingness to repurchase
2. Reluctance to switch
3. Likelihood to recommend

Additionally, a great customer experience can lead to increased revenues. Forrester found that companies that commit to improving the experience for their customers reported increases of up to $311 million in annual revenues for a $10 billion business—even when the improvements were only moderate.[1]

THE CUSTOMER EXPERIENCE

The customer experience encompasses all aspects of a customer's interaction with a company. It spans the sales, packaging, "out of box" experience (opening the product), registration, installation, setup and usage, and ongoing maintenance of the product or service (think computers). In a different example, the offline customer experience at a grocery store can include shelf displays, aisle width, shopping cart wheel malfunctions, employee interactions, restroom appearance, length of check-out lines, courtesy of clerks, ease of returns, even the size of the spaces in the parking lot. For a service, the customer experience spans the purchase, installation, usage, subscription, monthly bills, and any upgrades. The online customer experience can include Web site navigation, ease of finding information, Web site response time, and the number of clicks necessary to accomplish a task. All of these experiences can also include any social media interactions with the organization. Take a moment and think about what the customer experience means for your company and industry.

Now recall from Chapter 2 the discussion on customer life cycle. Many departments are responsible for the customer experience, including marketing, sales, R&D, manufacturing, customer service, field service, as well as training. The entire company plays a role in the customer experience, and each department has its own area of expertise, which must be brought "to the table" in the most effective way to produce the optimal customer experience.

When we understand our customers' wants and needs, we can begin to connect and interact with them throughout their customer life cycle based on what we have learned about them. We can use what we have learned to guide each area of the organization in how to best contribute to a great experience for each customer.

THE CUSTOMER PERSPECTIVE

An internal review of the customer experience needs to go further than just the touch points for which a single employee or team is responsible. It must look at the experience from the *customer's perspective* across *all touch points*. Only then can we be sure that we are firing on all cylinders and moving in the right direction for the customer.

A Tale of Two Airline Customer Experiences
The First

On a recent trip, my connecting flight was supposed to leave at about 9:00 PM. After a 10-minute delay, we were allowed to board; no sooner had we taken our seats when it was announced that there was a problem with a piece of the equipment and that mechanics were coming to fix it. "Please be patient and stay in your seats. . . ."

One hour later, the original problem had been fixed but two more had cropped up. The airline finally decided to let us get off the plane to stretch our legs. We stretched and paced for about 30 minutes, at which time the airline announced they would have to get another plane, because the right parts weren't available for this one. Airline crew began handing out vouchers for food in the airport, and we all scrambled to get one, since most of us were tired and hungry by now. I took mine to the closest shop, hoping to at least get some snacks and water, but I was told the vouchers were good only for food concessions and restaurants. One problem: All the concessions and restaurants were now closed! The vouchers were completely worthless.

If the airline had developed a customer experience strategy that considered this type of scenario (travel delays, as we all know, are not as rare as we would like them to be), how might it have done things differently? For one, the airline crew might have realized that the vouchers were not going to be of any use to us at that late hour. Then, as airline employees worked to acquire another plane for our flight, perhaps they could have found a carafe of coffee to serve us. Or, maybe, they could have had on hand special vouchers just for this type of occurrence, which would allow passengers to get a snack or bottled water at any shops still open at that late hour. Better still, knowing full well that travel is delayed at times, the airline might have planned ahead and stored some nonperishable snacks somewhere at the airport, to be accessed when it looked like a long delay was in the works.

A little bit of planning can go a long way when things don't work out the way they should.

The Second

I had been delayed on a Southwest Airlines flight due to low-lying fog, which meant we couldn't land at our intended destination, San Diego. We ended up being diverted 100 miles north, to Los Angeles.

Southwest Airlines personnel proved to be extremely helpful and friendly in this circumstance. Initially, they couldn't find a way to get us to San Diego, as all flights were grounded and no buses were available. As we gathered our carry-on bags, Southwest personnel announced that they had found buses. And somewhere, they had come up with a bunch of helium balloons, which they carried as they led us tired passengers down to baggage claim. More important, they kept us informed and cheerfully got us safely on to the buses in a very timely fashion. Although it was not a fun experience, Southwest personnel made it as pleasant and efficient as possible, for us *and* for them, with their quick thinking, cheerful attitude, and good service.

■ ■ ■

Traveling can be problematic any time of year. Airports are overcrowded, and people are anxious to get where they're going. Competition among the airlines, which is cutthroat these days, only makes things worse. In contrast to many, Southwest Airlines seems to have the processes and protocols down for improving the experience for its customers. While other airlines have made too many cuts in both service and quality,

Southwest has prioritized what is important for its passengers, and in this way it continues to provide a customer experience that matters to its customers. The airline hires people for their friendly, customer-focused attitudes, who are able to take their customers' perspective and offer good service with empathy and a smile. (More on Southwest Airlines in Chapter 11.)

In a world where customers can easily and quickly share the frustrating customer experiences they've had with brands and companies via social networks, enacting an effective customer experience strategy is *critical* for companies. Putting yourself in your customers' shoes and planning how to treat them in different scenarios helps improve the immediate, and future, customer experience. It also strengthens both your customer relationships and your brand image.

CUSTOMER EXPECTATIONS DRIVE THE OUTCOME

Understanding what customers expect to experience when they interact with your business is one of the keys to creating an experience that "rocks." Unless we understand the expectations of the customer experience from their perspective, we cannot begin to know whether we are meeting, much less exceeding, those expectations.

For example, customers in need of online customer service assistance generally have five specific expectations for that experience:

1. First and foremost, customers would prefer not to need a service experience at all. Far better if companies could prevent problems from ever taking place, by producing products that don't break down. That, of course, is unrealistic, and we must assume that problems will occur and need resolving. With that in mind, here are the other four customer expectations for an online service experience:
2. Customers want quick response times.
3. Customers want their problems solved—ideally, the first time.
4. Customers want to feel that the service person cares about them and their problems.
5. Customers need to be confident that using online service will be as easy, if not easier, than calling on the phone for assistance.

Organizations that offer online customer service should take these expectations into account when they are designing their online service experience across their Web site and social media touch points.

Set Customer Expectations

It is vital to set customer expectations. The more customers can stay informed, the greater the opportunity for customer satisfaction and delight, and the less room for complaints or criticisms. An excellent example of this is Domino's "Pizza Tracker." As soon as customers order a pizza online from Domino's, they are directed to a Web page where a horizontal bar tracks the progress of their order. At the top of the tracking bar are these labels: Order Placed, Prep, Bake, Quality Check, and Out for Delivery; the bar also displays the name of the employee who has been assigned to their order. The Tracker turns red as each stage of the pizza making is completed. It even asks customers for feedback about their assigned "delivery expert" and the overall experience.

By showing the Pizza Tracker on completion of an online order, Domino's is setting the customer's expectations for the experience. When I tried it, the process worked very nicely. Within 10 minutes of the "Your pizza just left the building" update, my doorbell rang; my pizza had arrived. The Domino's Pizza Tracker is impressive to watch and helps customers see what is happening with their order—plus, it's fun!

How does your organization help set customer expectations? Are customers kept in the dark about their purchase or usage experience? Talk to your customers, find out which part of your process they find difficult or frustrating, and then identify what you can do to fix it. Domino's did, and I am looking forward to ordering my next pizza from them.

Overcome What You Can't Control

In certain situations, it is important to set expectations to help customers through a part of the experience you *cannot* control. For example, parking lots and restroom facilities are often shared with several businesses and managed by a third party, such as in malls. Small parking spaces, or not enough of them, can cause frustration for customers who are coming to visit a professional office or retail store.

Recently, I ate at the Burger Bar in Las Vegas. The restaurant features delicious burgers, as well as specialty beers from around the world—the beer menu is extensive. In addition, fun beer signs are posted throughout the restaurant. When customers walk down the hall to the restroom (which is behind a door at the very end of the hall), they are taken on a visual tour of some of the many beers featured at Burger Bar.

Apparently, however, this restaurant shared its bathroom facilities with other stores and restaurants in the mall; as a result, its cool beer experience ended at the door. The hallway beyond the door was empty and painted a dull beige color. There were no beer signs; in fact, there was nothing on the walls at all. It was such a stark contrast to the interior of Burger Bar that it initially made me wonder whether I was in the right place! Sadly, the Burger Bar is stuck with this experience. Much like a communal parking lot, this bathroom situation was out of the establishment's control.

Let's ask ourselves what Burger Bar could have done to make the bathroom experience better for its customers. They couldn't change the shared bathrooms, but they could hang yet one more sign at the end of the hall, before the door leading out of Burger Bar, notifying customers that they are now leaving the restaurant and entering shared space. A sign might not completely remedy the situation, but sometimes simply setting expectations is all that is needed to turn an unpleasant experience into at least a tolerable one.

If you can't be in control of a situation (such as with shared bathrooms and parking lots), set expectations ahead of time, then make the best of what you *can* control. Once a company has formed strong relationships with its customers and established a loyal customer base, customers may complain but will most likely tolerate any minor inconveniences. Best-case scenario, they may be very forgiving and even defend the company when others criticize it. A loyal customer base will remain with the company—which is all-important in difficult economic times.

YOUR CUSTOMER EXPERIENCE COMPETITION

A question I am commonly asked is: "Who are the companies in my industry with best practices in customer experience?" The person asking this question is usually someone in marketing who wants to find out which companies to emulate when it comes to customer experience strategies. In fact, organizations should be asking a different question: Which are the companies with best practices in customer focus in *any* industry? Many benchmarking projects fall short of the mark because they do not look outside of their own world.

For example, I read a librarian's blog post about her organization's customer experience competition, in which she stated:

> Libraries need to rock, to be cool. Why? To survive . . . to thrive . . . to be valuable . . . to be essential for our customers. I have heard many librarians proclaim arrogantly that we are not in competition with the video store, the DVD store, Google, iTunes, and YouTube. But we are! WE ARE!

Clearly, this librarian recognizes that her customers have a lot of other media competing for their attention.

The best way to determine customer expectations of your organization's experience is to put yourself in your customers' shoes. Analyze what your experience looks like from their perspective. Then take a look at the experiences your competitors offer (companies that your customers may also be patronizing). Which of those experiences are better at meeting customer expectations? Which ones "rock"?

Unexpected Competition

While you're at it, analyze the other businesses your customers may also be frequenting, including their Web sites, social media, and offline interactions. For example, sites such as Apple iTunes and Amazon.com have interfaces that set expectations for the way many of us use the Web. These companies are competing with yours to offer the best customer experience, regardless of whether they are in the same industry as your organization. Even B2B customers are consumers in their off-hours, and their expectations of commercial businesses are affected by their interactions on sites that reward them with an outstanding consumer experience. You can learn a lot by researching which companies are doing it well, and which are not, from *your customer's perspective*.

UNCOVER THE BEST EXPERIENCE

Your customers are comparing experiences as they deal with top-notch customer-focused organizations. It is important to determine how your organization's customer experience stacks up against those other experiences your customers are having on both the business and the consumer sides. The following three steps will help you begin to plan the best experience for your customers:

Step 1: Look to your customers. By this, I mean find out what your customers expect from you and from other companies. What do they consider to be great customer service? What sets one experience apart from another in their minds? If you don't know the answers to these questions, ask! Your customers will tell you which companies they believe provide stellar (and not-so-stellar) customer experiences.

Step 2: Look in the mirror. Do detective work within your organization. What does it feel like to be your customer? Either do some "mystery shopping" or bring someone in who can do it for you with an unbiased perspective. Start with these questions:

- What is your organization's customer experience? Will it meet or exceed customer expectations?
- What happens when you call your customer service department?
- Where does the phone number listed in your marketing campaign really connect to?
- Do your Web sites direct customers to the right places?
- Are your social media activities creating an experience that is consistent with the rest of your brand?

Step 3: Look at competitors from your customer's perspective. Find out which organizations are competing for your customer's attention and dollars, both inside and outside your industry. How do their customer experiences compare to yours? Perhaps there isn't anyone in your industry yet who offers a standout customer experience; however, your consumers may have experienced outstanding customer service at, say, Nordstrom or Southwest Airlines. Your business clients may be serviced by Accenture, a management consulting, technology, and outsourcing organization that has been recognized as a leader in connecting with their customers by

Gartner and 1to1 Media.[2] How do the customer experiences in your industry compare to those your customers are having with award-winning organizations such as these?

Once you have done the legwork to understand customer expectations, audited your company's customer experience, as well as reviewed that of your customer experience competitors, you are ready to begin creating the experiences *your* customers want to have with your business. Planning the customer experience based on your customers' needs and expectations, as well as on best-in-class experiences both inside and outside your industry, will strengthen your brand and lay the foundation for stronger customer relationships.

FOCUS ON YOUR CUSTOMERS

The customer experience is considered by many companies to be one of the keys to unleashing the hidden power of their customers and differentiating themselves from their competitors. The ability to successfully manage the customer experience is the result of taking a customer-centric approach to business so that the customer is treated consistently well across all channels and throughout the customer life cycle.

A world-class customer experience strategy facilitates consistent treatment of customers, cultivates customer trust, and enables meaningful interactions at all touch points; most important, it meets and *exceeds* customer expectations. This is a customer experience that ignites passion, inspires brand loyalty, and cements relationships.

Chapter 6

GET THE LAY OF THE LAND

Managing the customer experience is not always an easy task. Expectations are set through many mechanisms: the brand, the staff, the experiences customers have with your competitors and even with other noncompeting brands and companies. Organizations that fall prey to performing "random acts of customer service" in their attempts to please customers can quickly end up exceeding their budget. Rather, what's needed to consistently meet and exceed customer expectations is a carefully orchestrated customer experience strategy, targeted usage of customer information, and solid execution.

MANAGING THE CUSTOMER EXPERIENCE—OR NOT

When an organization says it wants to "manage" the customer's experience, often it indicates the desire to design a perfectly branded encounter, every step of which moves the customer closer to the organization's goals. In short, the organization would like to be able to exert total control over the customer experience.

In actual practice, we can no more "manage" our customers' experience than we can control the rising of the sun. Our customers all have free will; they may choose to take the path we lay out for them or blaze their own trail. A better, far more reasonable and achievable goal is to ensure that each part of the customer experience is positive and helps meet customer goals as well as business goals.

Fortunately, even when customers choose to blaze their own trails, a business can learn a great deal about how those customers think, what their desires are, and how they want to be served. With that information in hand, organizations can respond by engaging and interacting with customers in a customized manner at each touch point. And subsequently, each time a customer engages with a business, the business can continue to learn about the best way to meet that customer's needs.

In this way, "managing" our company's customer experience becomes a strategy for the organization, ensuring that we engage with our customers in an optimal way at every opportunity. It gives us a structure from which we can capture important insights from those interactions, then use what we learn to help meet the needs of our customers at each and every place they come in contact with our organization. If we do this correctly, customers will be delighted with our interactions with them, they will continue to purchase from us, and, ideally, they will suggest to others that they do the same.

DESIGN THE CUSTOMER EXPERIENCE END-TO-END

I've said it before, but it bears repeating: Never leave the customer experience to chance. Your organization can create an experience that consistently meets your customers' needs *and* supports your brand.

To achieve that, you need to design a plan for how customers will engage with your business, across all the areas where they interact with you—the customer touch points with your organization and its people.

Crafting the Customer Experience

When you examine the customer experience you provide from your customers' point of view, you will likely find that they interact with your organization in various ways—some that you expect and some that you don't. "Customers Rock!" companies understand the various experiences of their customers and design improvements and make adjustments with them in mind—including how best to handle potential pain points.

Let's look at a laudable example of such a plan, "imagineered" (to use a Disney term) by Walt Disney Theme Parks. The following lists itemize a few of the concepts Disney has introduced in planning the theme park experience from a guest's (customer's) point of view.

Time Savers

- *FastPass:* This brilliant—and free—service allows guests to reserve a window of time for going on some of the most popular attractions. Guests receive a piece of paper, branded with a logo for each ride, that tells them when they can join the special FastPass queue. This queue puts them on the ride after little or no wait (even if the regular lines are very long). FastPass not only makes a family's visit more enjoyable, it also helps Disney better manage crowds.
- *PhotoPass:* This Disney service makes it more convenient for visitors to access their pictures taken by Disney photographers all around the parks. Instead of being handed a piece of paper with a number to look up at the end of the day (along with a lot of other people who are doing the same thing), guests receive a bar-coded card that stores a link to their photos. This card enables guests to print out their photos, have them burned onto a CD at the park, or access them via the Internet when they get home. For guests, PhotoPass saves them the hassle of getting that special shot framed just right; for Disney, it brings guests to the company Web site later to view and, hopefully, purchase photos: a win-win for both guests and company.

Convenience

- *Helping Hands on Rides:* This has to be the one accommodation I love the most about going on rides at Disney parks. On attractions where one's personal belongings could easily fall out of purses and pockets, such as roller-coasters and other thrill rides, Disney provides pouches on the back of each seat. The pouches, which close with Velcro for security, are large enough to hold a small purse or shopping bag. No more asking, "Could you please hold this for me?" or worrying about what will become of a bag you leave beside the ride. On the Silly Symphony Swings at Disney's California Adventure, shoes can easily fly off, so Disney has set up bins around the edges of the ride where guests can store their shoes "preflight." The concept of providing pouches and other containers for belongings really takes the guest's point of view into account and makes the experience even more enjoyable for them.

Surprises

- *Special Recognition:* If a Disney guest mentions to anyone at ticketing or in the Town Hall that it is someone's birthday celebration, a Disney employee (called a "cast member") gives the guest a special sticker or button with his or her name on it to wear for the day. Everywhere the guest goes in the parks that day, cast members wish the person a Happy Birthday!—usually by name, which can really make the guest feel as if a thousand friends remembered his or her special day. Disney offers similar stickers or buttons for couples on their honeymoon or celebrating an anniversary, as well as for first-time guests. People of all ages receive this special treatment, and sometimes a cast member will do something extra (such as serve a special dessert, sing a song, or offer a special seat on a ride) to help guests celebrate their special day, whatever it is. This park-wide recognition, along with other surprises that can occur along the way, makes the experience especially memorable for Disney guests who are marking an important milestone in their lives.

- *Hidden Mickeys:* There are Disney aficionados who have been to the park so many times that they have memorized every line spoken by every audio-animatronics figure in the attractions. What can Disney possibly do to keep these guests excited? Hide Mickeys! Here's how it works: Disney Imagineers conceal images of Mickey (most often a silhouette of his famous ears) as they finalize a ride, providing much fodder for guests as they look for them throughout the many Disney parks. When Disney fanatics find the images and point them out to the uninitiated, they feel like part of the "inside team"; it also adds an extra dimension to the Disney guest experience.

- *Theming:* Disney has even carefully considered how guests traverse its parks. For example, each "land" at the Disneyland theme park has a different surface underfoot, so guests can actually feel the transition from one to another under their feet. Disney's California Adventure doesn't do this to the same extent, but guests can easily recognize the transition from one part of "California" to another by noting the logos on the trash cans (which are everywhere).

Design Considerations

Disney Theme Parks and Resorts spends time listening to its guests so it can deeply understand what would make the park visit a better experience for guests in the future. The company has adapted its business processes to plan for and solve real and perceived customer pain points—in addition to sprinkling a little pixie dust along the way to make the whole experience a delight. By putting forth similar thought and effort, your organization can devise equally enjoyable encounters for your customers. The following sections suggest considerations to take into account when designing your own brand's customer experience.

Make It Meaningful

It is a constant challenge to make each customer interaction unique, memorable, and relevant to *that customer at that moment in time.* What your brand signifies to me is, undoubtedly, very different from what it means to my colleague, sister, or friend. Fortunately, digital media enables companies to be extremely flexible in how they can differentiate online customer experiences based on individual needs and values. It also allows brands to make these experiences fun and engaging. Successful brands operating in the digital world are the ones that tailor these experiences to their customers, as well as interact with and engage customers in a way that is meaningful for both the company and the customers.

Make It Consistent

One of the most important ingredients in building customer loyalty is providing a consistent customer experience. Yet, often one of the most frustrating aspects for customers when they interact with a company is the inconsistent treatment they receive at different touch points within the organization.

Customers want to have the same positive experience whether they are interacting with your sales teams, marketing materials, customer service agents, or social media sites. Inconsistent experiences lead to customer statements such as, "My doctor is very knowledgeable, and I trust him. However, his office administrative team isn't very helpful and is almost unfriendly. Maybe I will switch doctors...."

Consistency is especially important to customers who are part of a VIP or loyalty program but aren't recognized as such across the business. I have had the privilege of attending some amazing VIP hospitality events put together for customers. One I recall in particular was at a golf tournament, where a car manufacturer had set up a hospitality area exclusively for owners of a certain make of car. The manufacturer's corporate offices made sure the "owner experience" it presented at the tournament was excellent in every way possible, in order to positively contribute to the overall brand experience. However, what happened after the event was over? As I mentioned, consistency is key. The organization needed to ensure the same VIP experience was extended to every future customer interaction with that brand for those owners: in the Service and Parts department, with sales managers, via any e-mails and marketing pieces, and at every single customer touch point at every dealer. This type of special program requires that you recognize your VIP customers at all touch points, not just at special events. It also requires coordination of VIP treatment across internal functional areas and effective collaboration with partners (in this case, the dealerships).

Is all of this doable? Yes—but it requires planning, followed by flawless execution. Customers have high expectations. The companies that can create consistent, memorable customer experiences will have an edge. Is your company one of them?

Make the Experience Part of a Story

The story we tell our customers and clients is part of the experience. This could be the story of your brand or a story that involves the customer's motivations for interacting with you. For example, I'm not just buying dog food; I am buying my pet's health and happiness. I am not just procuring printing services for the office; I am helping us focus on our core competencies. Disney is very good at this; each attraction and area inside the Disney theme parks is designed to tell a backstory about that area, in quite a bit of detail. What story are you telling your customers?

Appeal to the Senses

A customer experience can be impacted by the smells, sights, and sounds around us, especially in consumer-facing businesses. For example, according to scientific research, smell can evoke memories from long ago, which means aromas can be powerfully associated with people, places, and incidents from our past.[1]

One of my favorite positive examples is the smell of freshly ground coffee at Starbucks, which the company views as part of the customer experience. Similarly, realtors burn vanilla-scented candles when hosting open houses. Bakeries blow the smell of freshly baked goods into the shopping mall. Car washes infuse that "new car smell" into customer vehicles to make them seem fresh again. In these ways and others, aromas can become part of the positive brand experience.

Conversely, scents also can result in a poor customer experience. When my family and I were shopping around for an orthodontist for my children, we narrowed down the field to two candidates and made introductory appointments with each of them. One of the reasons we didn't choose the first candidate was reflected in the words of my son: "Mom, he had really bad breath!" Sweet-smelling breath should be the first thing any dentist or orthodontist should have!

Hotels have been using aromas for many years and often pipe them throughout their lobbies and common areas. According to one hotel chain that uses scent in its lobbies to evoke a feeling of calm, the aroma is part of "delivering an arrival experience." Will guests recall their stay at one of these hotels when they catch a whiff of the same scent the next time? Will it help them feel more at home when they stay at these hotels? Either way, companies need to understand how to use scent, and how the customer will remember the experience associated with that scent (good or bad).

When you are reviewing your customer experience, it is important to consider *all* of the senses. What do your customers feel, taste, smell, see, and hear when they interact with your company? What do you want them to experience? Planning the encounter all the way down to the senses, possibly even designing different experiences for different customers, is one of the keys to a successful customer strategy.

Pay Attention to the Details

Whether yours is a retail establishment, a restaurant, a service, a small business, or a large corporation, every detail of your customer experience speaks volumes about your brand, your organization's culture, and the way you conduct your business. For example, if you have a brick-and-mortar presence, even something such as the appearance of company restrooms, can enhance or detract from the customer experience. While you certainly don't need to decorate restrooms with the type of amenities you might find in an upscale hotel, you do need to meet the basic requirements: ensure that the restrooms are neat and clean, that all necessary supplies are refilled on a regular basis, and that appropriate services are available to help meet your customer's needs (purse hooks for ladies, for example).

You can even go a bit further and make your restrooms (or waiting room or other common space) a direct reflection of your brand or business. Carry through the same decorative theme as in the rest of your facility. Add a small "surprise" to delight your customers, such as a sign, a nicely framed photo or picture, or an attractive color scheme. For example, casual-dining Italian restaurant Macaroni Grill plays "learn to speak Italian" lessons over the bathroom speakers instead of music.

Customers will notice when you pay attention to even the smallest details. Whatever you decide to do, don't treat your common spaces as afterthoughts, or your customers may decide they don't want to think about you anymore, either.

MAP THE CUSTOMER JOURNEY

When you engage in disciplined planning and analysis, the result will be an improved customer experience. Placing a few first-rate customer service representatives at key customer touch points probably isn't enough by itself to make a long-term difference for your customers or your company. To craft a consistently outstanding customer experience, you need to strategically plan how the company will engage with customers across all points of customer contact. Every interaction or "golden moment" with customers contributes to the overall customer experience and leaves brand impressions.

It is imperative to understand how each of these touch points affects the customer's interactions with your organization. To achieve this depth of understanding, many companies use a *customer experience map* as a tool to determine what their customer experience looks like.

Unfolding the Map

Mapping the customer experience is a process that takes the customer's perspective and examines all actions a customer must take to accomplish his or her task or goal. Like a road map, the customer journey is charted to identify all areas of customer interaction with a company. In general, this process of creating a customer experience map has five main steps:

1. Map the *current* experience of your customers.
2. Understand the *points of strength and weakness* in the experience.
3. Craft the *desired* customer experience based on customer needs, preferences, and behaviors, as well as business goals.
4. *Identify and improve* key parts of the customer experience to move it closer to the desired experience.
5. *Measure* the customer experience to make sure it rocks.

By using the customer point of view to map the current customer experience, organizations can see their business as their customers do. It is also helpful in several other ways.

Discover Customer Pain Points

Mapping the customer experience quickly reveals where customers struggle with a company's processes or requirements. For example, customers don't enjoy having to repeat their account information if they have to be passed from one person to another in a call center. While some of this may be unavoidable in certain regulated industries, looking at the process from the customer's perspective highlights these repetitious areas and helps the company identify where its customers may be getting frustrated. Once these areas of potential customer frustration have been identified, employees can show a little bit of extra empathy when dealing with customers at those sensitive touch points.

Leverage What Is Working

A customer experience map also helps illustrate where the best practices in customer interactions are being used in the organization; these can then be shared and used to improve other company touch points.

Understand Customer Motivators

By looking at each point of interaction along the customer's journey, your company gains insight into what customers value and want to accomplish by doing business with you. This information comes not only from what customers share at each of these touch points but also from the choices they make as they strive to fulfill their needs through their interactions.

Mapping the current customer experience paves the way for companies to craft the best experience at each touch point. The effort applied to improve each area will depend on the prioritization of that touch point, based on both the importance of the customer activity as well as the level of improvement needed. In addition, organizations with comprehensive customer data and a solid understanding of customer needs can pair the insights gleaned from the customer experience map with what they know about each individual customer to create a more personalized experience at critical touch points. Companies can learn continuously from each interaction with a customer and iterate improvements on a regular basis.

Since the customer experience spans all functional areas of a business, it is important to gain buy-in and support from the management team. Get executives and managers involved in the process as early as possible to help decide on the criteria for prioritizing outcomes, review the findings along the way, and take what they learn back to their teams so improvements can be introduced that will benefit the customer—and, ultimately, the company.

Customer GPS

As you might expect, I don't recommend sitting in a conference room and mapping out your company's customer experience journey without first talking to customers. Most organizations already have some important insights about the customer journey (via their sales, market research, and customer service teams), but this knowledge must be supplemented with actual customer input. Therefore, it is important to tune into your "customer GPS"—to locate where your customers are in their experience with your organization.

Any information gaps can be filled in via various methods commonly used to collect the "voice of the customer" (VOC) and previously discussed in Chapter 2. These methods include ethnographic-type studies, direct customer interviews, usability studies (if the product or service lends itself to that), mystery shopping, surveys, and social media listening. Online communities, forums in particular, can often yield fairly detailed insights. The methods your company uses will vary based on what it already knows about its customers, their needs, and their levels of satisfaction at different touch points.

Drawing the Map

Once most of the customer experience journey has been described through one or more of the methods described here, it's time to draw the map. Customer experience maps are typically laid out according to the customer life cycle (refer back to Chapter 2 for more on this topic). In other words, the map illustrates where and how customers touch the company at each stage of their life cycle with that organization. Some of the life-cycle stages, such as Usage, will be broken out into more detailed sets of activities.

Customer experience touch maps can be created using a variety of visual styles. The following information, which is found on most maps, is described using a customer renewing a magazine subscription as an illustration:

- *Activity:* Who is the customer (loyal, new, VIP)? In what activity or task is the customer engaged? What is the customer trying to accomplish or achieve via this activity?

  Example: The customer—let's call her Joan—wants to renew a magazine subscription.
- *Touch point:* Where does Joan need to "touch" or interact with the company to accomplish this task? Who does she interact with, if anyone, for this activity? If data is being collected or shared, what is it and where does it go within the company?

  Example: Joan calls the toll-free number to renew her subscription.
- *Path:* Where was Joan before she tried to accomplish this activity? Was prior data collected about her that is needed now? If the activity is successful, what does Joan do next? Where does she go if there is a problem completing the activity? What if she needs additional help?

  Example: Joan found the toll-free number on the bottom of her renewal bill. Her account number will need to be provided. Other information from the bill also may be needed in order to complete the transaction. If Joan is successful, her magazine will be renewed, and she will receive a confirmation e-mail.

- *Customer emotions:* How does Joan feel after interacting at this touch point (good/bad/neutral)? Is she more or less satisfied than she was before?

  Example: Joan might feel good if she was sincerely thanked during the interaction. She might feel neutral if her interaction was processed as nothing more than a transaction. And she might be upset if her credit card was denied.

- *Assessment:* Is this touch point a customer pain point, an opportunity for a new process or interaction, a company best practice, or something else?

  Example: This will depend on the company.

Reach for the Destination

Once you have completed the customer experience touch map, it's time to take a critical look at what it reveals:

- Highlight and celebrate best practice areas that result in positive customer touch points; apply these to other customer touch points, where possible.
- Develop criteria to help prioritize any opportunities for improvement.
- Identify customer pain points, and brainstorm ideas for new processes that were uncovered during the mapping.

The desired or ideal customer experience can be created from the output of this review, along with an execution plan.

Once the plan is laid out, all parts of the organization must participate to make it a reality. Keep in mind that the customer experience plan can't be static. Just as annual updates are made to road maps, you will need to make regular revisions or changes to your company's customer experience map. Some of these may be significant, say if a major change is introduced in the way your business goes about accomplishing its goals; others may require only minor tune-ups. By constantly listening to and learning from customers, organizations can discover how best to tweak and customize the customer experience. With customers as your tour guide, the experience may always be changing, but it will also be rewarding.

Chapter 7

FINE-TUNE THE EXPERIENCE

L et's briefly look at Disney again. Per the company, nearly 80,000 people visit its parks daily; on average, each guest has 60 interactions with Disney cast members per day, which translates into 60 opportunities to make or break the customer experience. Unfortunately, even if 59 of these cast member interactions are exemplary, but number 60 is terrible, it is number 60 that the customer will go home and talk about.

To prepare for this possibility, Disney takes a proactive approach, using experience mapping (described in Chapter 6) to identify all points of contact with its customers. Managers look at the experience through the eyes of the customer, and then they align the organization's strengths with guest interactions, or "moments of magic."

What happens if a customer exchange is negative? According to a study by RightNow Technologies, a customer experience management company, poor experiences are more likely to be shared across a customer's social network.[1] Its research indicates that 79 percent of customers who had a bad experience with a company told others about it. In addition, 97 percent used word of mouth, including social media, as their preferred method of sharing. These statistics show that now more than ever, companies need to take a very close look at their customer experience and make sure that it "rocks" at each step along the way.

This can be achieved by continuously fine-tuning the experience for your customers. To make the most of a customer's experience with your organization, first ensure that you craft a solid introductory experience for each customer; next, customize the touch points of the experience to meet their personal needs and preferences, when possible; and, third, make sure each interaction evokes a positive customer response.

TAKE CARE OF THE BEGINNING

In many ways, the most important part of your relationship with the customer begins *right after* the sale. The first month or so of that relationship sets the tone for what the customer might expect in the months and years to come. For this reason, many companies put an official customer experience program in place for the first 30 days.

As an example, one domain registration company staffs a New Customer Orientation team whose members personally call each new client, then follow up with e-mails. Regardless of the price of the products purchased, employees make contact with each new customer to understand what that customer is trying to accomplish and see how the company can help. This is *not* a sales pitch; it's a way to provide a resource for their new customers.

In another example, Salesforce.com offers a short Webinar series for new customers to introduce them to the firm's online community and give them resources for getting started and receiving help. Other companies create welcome kits to thank customers and let them know how best to interact with the company going forward.

Tips for Making the Most of the First Month

Here are some tips for welcoming new customers into the fold:

- *Make the first contact.* Contact new customers and let them know you are glad they have chosen to do business with you. This is especially important for customers with whom you expect to have a long-term relationship. New customer contact is most effective by phone, but you can also do it with a thank-you card (preferably, handwritten, if volumes allow) or an e-mail message. If customers use social media as their primary communication channel, connect with them via those sites and say hello.

- *Get to know them.* Spend time with new customers to learn how they will use your product or service. This will help you better assist them, and it will also help to develop the trust that is so important to a relationship.
- *Be personal.* If possible, give new customers a personal contact in your company, an individual they can talk to should any questions or issues arise. If they will be dealing with multiple contacts, provide a quick reference card with everyone's contact information and organizational responsibilities (written from the customer's point of view) so customers know how to get things done most effectively at your company.
- *Follow up.* Make a point of connecting with customers a few times during their first 30 days with your company. This is especially important for valuable customers, business customers, and those who have purchased a big-ticket item from your company. Send them a small token of your appreciation, if possible; if gifts are precluded, a donation to a nonprofit is often acceptable. Call just to see how they are doing. Let customers know your company wants to help them be successful. Most importantly, tell new customers that you care about them and that you are glad they are your customers!

MAKE IT PERSONAL

You can use your understanding of your customer's needs and motivators to help create a more relevant, personal experience for them. When you tailor the customer experience based on individual preferences, you build trust and loyalty and encourage positive word of mouth. Often, you can collaborate with customers to ensure that you're designing the experience exactly the way they want it.

One example of a company successfully using personalization to better connect with its guests is Hilton Hotels, a chain that has rolled out a number of ways to customize its offerings to guest needs. For one, the Hilton Breakfast is offered as part of the hotel buffet and room service. Breakfast makes up a large percentage of the meals eaten at a hotel, and

Hilton is reaching out to its customers to encourage more of them to eat it there. Hilton introduced the Hilton Breakfast in 2007, under this premise: "Everyone's idea of the perfect breakfast is *different*." Hilton's brochure describes the program this way: "Simply select the breakfast that's right for you, and follow the color chosen on the Hilton breakfast buffet. We'll do the rest—you'll find that our buffet offers the widest choice of fresh and premium quality product imaginable."

More specifically, the contents of Hilton's breakfast buffet are color-coded into these categories: Low Fat & Low Calorie, Hi-Energy, High Fiber, Low Cholesterol, and Indulgence (i.e., everything on the menu). Guests can self-select their food preferences and co-create a personalized customer experience based on their needs, which may differ from one Hilton stay to another.

Hilton also allows guests to customize their hotel stay with the Suite Selection program. Offered by Hilton's Homewood Suites brand, Suite Selection was launched in 2008 as a response to guest requests. Homewood Suites found that they had many repeat guests who asked for the option to choose their own rooms. Hilton thought, if you can choose your seat on an airplane, why *not* be able to choose your own room?

The Suite Selector is an interactive online tool that allows any guest who wants to reserve a Homewood Suites room to view the locations of the spaces available by looking at hotel floor plans. Hilton HHonors members (Hilton's loyalty program) are given the additional privilege of choosing the exact suite location when they use Hilton's eCheck-in service. This service provides a significant benefit to anyone who is a frequent traveler or has specific needs with respect to hotel room locations (for example, away from elevators or ice machines). My family and I used the Suite Selector to choose a particular suite when we traveled with our dog. We were able to select a room at the far end of the hall on the top floor, where any pet noises coming from our suite would bother as few other hotel guests as possible. What peace of mind that gave us!

Customizing the experience for and with your customers doesn't have to be difficult. To help deliver a memorable experience, you have to recognize your customer's needs, be flexible in delivering the experience, and make customer preferences and requirements available to the appropriate people across the organization.

YOU ARE ALWAYS ONSTAGE

Recently, I was one of only a few people sitting in a local branch of a major-brand coffee shop (no, not Starbucks), when I overheard a loud conversation coming from *behind* the counter. It went something like this:

Wow, can you believe three limos of high school students pulled up the other night after their dance and we had to make a whole bunch of lattes, iced teas, and frozen drinks? It took *forever* to close!

It continued:

Some huge PTA group came in the other night at 8:30 and promised they would help put the chairs back when they were done. They finally left at 9:00, and the place was a mess. We didn't get out of here for ages that night. How rude.

And finally:

Julie was in here and was so drunk we had to close the doors early and put chairs in front of them so no one would come in.

I was very tempted to stand up and say, "Hey, guys and gals, I write about the customer experience, and I am not too impressed with yours right now!" I don't think they realized that *every word they were saying reflected on the business.* Based on what they said, none of these employees seemed willing to put in a little extra effort to service large, late-night orders, because it might inconvenience them. Just as disappointing, they didn't seem to care (or even notice) that I was there and could hear them talking; they were too busy having their own "social hour" behind the counter.

Here is another example, which I heard the other day spoken by a cashier at a grocery store (another large chain, by the way): "Can I get a bagger over here? You aren't paying me enough to have me bag the groceries, too!" I heard this comment as I was approaching the checkout counter with my few purchases. Wow, I wondered, what does *that* do to the brand's marketing messages?

My point is this: A business can spend a lot of money building its brand and designing a cool logo. It can market the latest specials to all its local customers. It can sponsor an engaging social media site and introduce a fabulous loyalty program to reward its best customers. But if the company's employees are not doing their part to support the customer experience, all those efforts will be a waste of money.

The customer experience incorporates what every employee is doing every minute—*even when no one is there to appreciate it.* Employees are "onstage" whenever they are in any area where their customers (or guests) can see or hear them. Customer perception is a critical component of deciding whether an experience with a company is positive or negative. Every employee contributes to that perception, at every interaction, regardless of whether they are behind the counter, on the phone, on the accounts payable team, or on the cleaning crew.

That is why it's so crucial to hire employees who have a passion for serving others. Then treat them like gold, and they will take care of your customers. Remind them all that anytime they are potentially visible or within earshot of customers, they are still "onstage" and are actively participating in the customer experience.

PUTTING IT ALL TOGETHER FOR THE CUSTOMER

A Walk through a Car Dealer Experience

Car dealers are the face of an automotive company's corporate brand to customers. They are in charge of local customer treatment and even have some flexibility in what they can offer, especially when it comes to building customer loyalty. However, some car dealers focus so intently on short-term measures—mainly sales—that they fail to provide a dealership experience that will bring customers back for more. In addition, many dealerships are located along a town's "auto row," among numerous competitors, where the goal is to keep the customer on the lot or in the showroom and out of a competitor's shop.

As a result, visits to car dealerships do not always result in positive customer feedback. Listen in on some of the comments frequently heard from customers at dealerships:

"I dread the hard sell at the dealership."
"I don't want to endure that kind of psychological warfare."
"I am investing in a 5-to-10-year experience; who I buy from is critical."

Meanwhile, a growing number of customers are turning to the Internet to ease their car-buying experience. The Internet sales department of many car dealerships provides a no-haggle experience; they can transmit prices quickly, by e-mail or by phone.

Once customers become loyal to a brand, many of them return to buy from that car manufacturer again and again over the years. Even children are influenced by the kind of car their parents drive, so owner loyalty is very important for car manufacturers. But what drives it (so to speak)? And what can car dealerships do to improve it?

The car dealership customer experience can teach all companies some valuable lessons in how to view the customer experience from an outside perspective and then fine-tune it to better meet customer needs. Let's look at two of the main parts of the customer life cycle—buying and maintaining a vehicle.

The Buying Experience

Lesson 1: Make it easy for customers to buy from you. Internet sales departments are one way to offer a no-hassle method to buy cars, thus improving the customer's brand perception when they come in to sign the papers.

Lesson 2: Understand the buying experience from your customer's point of view. Map out what it looks and feels like when a customer comes in to your dealership—from the test drive to the negotiation to the purchase and financing. Where are the snags? When do long waiting periods occur? Customers who have a positive experience are more likely to come back for service in the future and to tell their friends and family about the dealership.

Lesson 3: Thank your customer for buying. Gift-after-purchase programs can surprise and delight customers. Here are some tidbits from a customer survey of one of these programs:

* 75 percent of recipients told others about the gift.
* 30 percent of those told four to seven additional people.
* 98 percent would recommend the brand to others.
* 71 percent said the gift exceeded their expectations.[2]

Lesson 4: Make sure the first 30 days of ownership are a great experience. Customers want to be reassured that they have made the right decision. Creating a "First 30 Days" program could include a thank-you, as mentioned; a DVD sent to new owners, highlighting car features with "how-to-use" lessons; offers for a free car wash and oil change; and whatever else local customers would consider worthwhile to help bring them back in to the dealership.

The Service Experience

Most customer interactions with a car dealership are made in one place: the service department. Service typically results in repeat business, meaning this is an ongoing revenue stream for dealers, as well as an opportunity to strengthen the relationship with car owners. Customers care about one thing: getting their car back quickly and in good shape.

Lesson 5: Set customer expectations in the service department. Make sure customers know what they can expect when they bring in their car for service—including estimated wait time before seeing a service representative, estimated time to perform the maintenance or repair, impact on their day, and potential costs.

The service advisor's role is a key factor in creating a positive customer experience. If a service advisor spends time with the car owner to help set expectations and explains the services performed after they are completed, customer satisfaction and loyalty increase. Research from J.D. Power and Associates, a consumer research firm, found that customers who were delighted by the explanations of the car dealer service staff were more likely to be loyal—even when their repair was not completed correctly the first time:[3]

- 72 percent said that they would definitely return to the dealer for service covered under warranty, compared with only 42 percent of customers who were only satisfied or indifferent.
- Nearly half (47 percent) of delighted customers reported that they would definitely return to the dealer for maintenance or repairs that they would have to pay for, compared with only 17 percent of those customers who were satisfied or indifferent.

Lesson 6: Your employees make a world of difference. Customers develop trust in a dealership when they experience consistency in their interactions there. If they see the same service advisor time after time, they begin to feel that they are part of a valuable relationship. Therefore, employee retention in the service department is critical to customer retention and future sales.

Lesson 7: Create an outstanding service experience. Customers want to have their car serviced as quickly as possible while minimizing the inconvenience. Dealerships can make the service experience easier for customers in various ways, notably the following:

- Offer rides to pick up or drop off customers or their cars.
- Offer loaner cars for longer maintenance or repairs.
- Return the customer's car clean, both inside and out.
- Provide an area where customers can wait comfortably, make phone calls, log on to the Internet, or grab a cup of coffee.

Key Takeaways

- The sale is not the end of the relationship with a customer; it's the beginning. How can car dealerships, as well as other businesses, create customers for life? Focus on the customer, meet their needs, and develop trust by doing what you say you will do, when you say you will do it.
- Make it as easy and enjoyable as possible for them to do business with you.
- Ensure that the customer is thrilled in their first 30 days of ownership, and beyond.
- Orchestrate a fabulous and memorable experience each time the customer interacts with your brand (in person or online), for whatever reason.

A COMPETITIVE DIFFERENTIATOR

Companies that embrace the customer experience as a competitive differentiator are already a step ahead of their competitors. These companies become the measuring rod for all other experiences. You design a customer experience that rocks when you plan an effective customer strategy, understand customer expectations and needs, use that understanding to fine-tune the experience for your customers, and continually improve and learn from customer interactions and best practices. Is your organization setting the pace, or is it still trying to catch up?

Case Study
Lexus Treats Customers as Guests in Their Home

The Lexus Covenant

> Lexus will enter the most competitive,
> prestigious automobile race in the world.
> Over 50 years of Toyota automotive
> experience has culminated in the creation
> of Lexus cars. They will be the
> finest cars ever built.
> Lexus will win the race because:
> Lexus will do it right from the start.
> Lexus will have the finest dealer network
> in the industry. Lexus will treat each
> customer as we would a guest in our home.
> If you think you can't, you won't . . .
> If you think you can, you will!
> We can, we will.

The Lexus Covenant and Culture

"In August of 1987, Lexus Division Managers and Associates committed themselves to providing the highest levels of product quality and customer service." Thus begins the guiding document for the culture at luxury automaker Lexus. The Lexus Covenant is printed on wallet-sized cards that associates carry with them, as well as on posters, brochures, and pictures throughout Lexus. Al Smith, the VP of Customer Services for Lexus Division, explained that the Lexus Covenant drives everything they do at Lexus: "We are committed to making the best cars, selecting the best dealers, and treating each customer as a guest in our own home."

This thinking permeates the culture at Lexus, as well as the culture at each of its dealers, and it is meticulously supported in every aspect of the business. Extensive training, which includes ongoing instruction on the Lexus Covenant, is provided for any Lexus associate who comes in contact with the customer. Dealers were handpicked when the brand was started, which gave Lexus the advantage of choosing those who were already customer-sensitive. The focus on the customer is reflected in the measures that Lexus uses to track satisfaction with sales, service, and product dependability. Lexus surveys every customer, and these metrics are tied back to how dealers are managed and rewarded.

According to Smith, the customer experience is the number one most important area for Lexus. Smith explains that since the company has a relatively small and exclusive dealer network, they are better able to ensure a consistently outstanding customer experience. Many car buyers don't really distinguish between talking to the dealer versus talking to corporate headquarters; they just want the experience to be consistent. Most touch points are actually with the dealerships, so anytime Lexus is delivering on a request for a customer, Lexus makes sure to work with the dealers to be the point of delivery.

Lexus treats each customer uniquely, and associates are given a general understanding of what to look for in customers (based on whether they are loyal, new, etc.). They do not receive any particular monetary guidelines; rather, they seek to identify "the best way to say yes" to customer requests. Because Lexus was able to set up the company to be customer-focused from the very beginning, it has shown that by doing what's right for the customer, profitability improves.

Welcoming Customers

Lexus has a series of customer-facing programs, including the Lexus Owner Welcome Program. Within two to four weeks of purchasing a Lexus, the new owner is invited to a special welcome event. This event takes place in the evening at the dealership, and all key dealer personnel, including sales, service, the general manager, design specialists, and technology gurus are there to give presentations, answer questions, and get to know the customers. Food and wine are served, and it's a nice start to a long relationship.

About 45 to 90 days after purchase, Lexus associates contact customers to gather feedback on how things are going with their cars.

(continued)

(*continued*)

At every other touch point thereafter, customers are surveyed about their most recent interactions. This process is maintained across the lifetime of the relationship. The information is stored in a national database, making it possible for any customer to interact anywhere within the Lexus family and know their history will be available to Lexus associates, who can then better manage the relationship.

Other customer-facing programs include a robust online experience for Lexus owners. They can make payments and schedule service appointments online; the Web site helps set expectations for how they will be contacted about their service and how to set up a loaner car. According to Smith, these programs have been very successful, and Lexus works hard to remain sensitive to customer concerns throughout all touch points.

Using Social Media to Care for Customers

Lexus is always working on new ways to improve the customer experience and usually finds that the most robust ideas come from the customers themselves. About a year ago, conversations with dealers revealed that some of the younger Lexus customers spent time on social networking sites such as Facebook and Twitter while they waited in the lounges. These customers also informed dealers that they would like to use social networking to talk with Lexus, in addition to talking with their friends on these sites.

Lexus realized that if customers were talking about the company online, it needed to be present and participate wherever customers chose to share. To that end, its social media team, composed of four people, actively watches and listens to customer conversations. When it's appropriate, they also engage and introduce themselves as Lexus representatives. They are especially proactive in their approach to customer service, and they get dealers involved where it makes sense. For example, if a conversation were taking place with a customer on Facebook regarding a service issue, the social media rep would listen to and capture that information, contact the customer, then work with the dealer and the customer to resolve the issue. Ideally, a customer would then share via social media how quickly and efficiently that issue was settled. The Lexus team is very excited about their social media activity and expects to continue interacting wherever customers want them to.

It's about People

Smith shared that at the end of the day, it's really the Lexus associates who are providing the customer experience: "If you empower your associates, you will win every time." Smith is convinced that this is the best way to deliver on your commitments, as long as you stay authentic with customers, deliver consistently, and have trust in and respect for the customer.

Information taken from a personal interview with Al Smith on January 13, 2011.

Chapter 8

ALIGN AROUND THE CUSTOMER

What does the process of *aligning around the customer* mean for organizations? It means designing business processes to benefit the customer, not just the business. It means coordinating interactions with the customer across multiple touch points. It means co-designing the experience with the customers, to make it the way *they* want it.

NO SILOS

Customers don't, or can't, always differentiate between a company's internal departments. Regardless of medium or origin, all of a customer's experiences with a company add up to communicate the brand to the customer. Too often in companies, however, sales, marketing, social media, and customer service are managed separately in organizational "silos" or are outsourced. The employees in the various departments may not see or speak to each other regularly, or at all, they may keep their customer data in different systems, and they may not use common metrics to help them drive a consistent experience.

From the company's perspective, "silo thinking" looks like this: Each department is focused on providing the customer experience from its perspective, using its own success measures. But when we look at an organization from the customer's perspective, what should we see? One unified brand with everyone working together to ensure a memorable customer experience. That is not always the case. A company's customers may have numerous interactions that seem to reflect many brands, each resulting in a different experience (and often based on how employees are instructed to behave).

Are the messages of one department or team speaking more loudly to customers of your organization than another? Do you need to bring these messages into alignment? What do customers think about your brand, from all perspectives? These are critical questions to ask as your company considers how to develop a cohesive strategy that produces an aligned customer experience, regardless of where the customer touches the organization.

Who "Owns" the Customer?

Many companies have an undeclared war going on between sales and marketing. Sales complains that marketing doesn't bring them any good leads. Marketing complains that they feel like second-class citizens and that sales doesn't follow up on all the valuable leads they give them. Who wins this war? No one. Who loses? Both the customer *and* the company.

Earlier in my career, I headed up B2B marketing for a large technology company in the United Kingdom, and our sales and marketing groups were supposed to collaborate. Instead, they complained about each other. Only after I spent time talking one-on-one with the sales managers, sales reps, and the members of my marketing team did we manage to break down the walls blocking effective collaboration.

I assigned one marketing person to each sales district in order to become fully ingrained with the sales team. And to better understand how to meet the needs of both the customer and the sales team, the marketers attended sales meetings, ate their meals with the sales teams, and went on customer visits with their sales counterparts.

Within only a few months of focusing on the needs of the sales organization, the marketers came to be seen as integral players on the sales teams. They were invited to off-site sales meetings and asked for their ideas. They were invited to sales team Christmas parties and were treated as "one of us." They essentially became an extended arm of the sales team. The result: Our business unit beat quota that year, for the first time in quite a while—and we did it as a united team.

Working Together

Customers want to be approached by this kind of cohesive team. They don't want to feel stuck in the middle of a company squabble; they want a unified organization that is ready and willing to meet their needs.

So, who "owns" the customer? Really, no one at any company owns the customer; the customers own themselves. They are in charge of whether or not they continue to do business with a company. They choose which path to take in the customer experience. In short, the customer is in charge of the relationship with the company.

To maintain this relationship, all company functions need to work together, especially in a large organization where it's often more difficult to coordinate customer touch points. The goal is to understand the customer so thoroughly that everyone wins—the company *and* the customer. Only then will organizational teams be able to collaborate successfully across departments to understand, create, and maintain the desired customer experience.

What is required to make this goal a reality? The customer experience needs to be managed as a cross-functional initiative, headed up by a strong executive sponsor or champion who will ensure the program is embraced throughout the organization. The right processes then need to be introduced, along with consistent measures across the company to drive supporting behaviors. These processes have to work well within the company; more importantly, they must work for the customer.

DESIGN PROCESSES THAT FIT

When my family first moved to our current city, we found ourselves in urgent need of a primary care physician for a sick family member. Needless to say, I wasn't familiar yet with the doctors in our area, so I asked a good friend for a recommendation. Here was our experience.

Doctor 1: Recommended

After calling the office of this doctor, I spent 20 minutes on hold before reaching a live person. The woman who finally answered the phone was fairly abrupt and matter-of-fact with me. Because we were new patients, I was told my sick family member would be required to make a 30-minute "new patient" appointment (as opposed to a regular office visit) before he could be seen for anything else. For that intake appointment, we were asked to show up 30 minutes early to fill out all the new-patient paperwork. At this point, the receptionist checked the intake appointments for the next schedule before informing me that the doctor was fully booked for two days! When I objected, stressing the urgency of the situation, she referred me to the local urgent care clinic. I thanked her and hung up.

Doctor 2: Found Online

I found the second doctor online. On calling his office, I spent about three minutes on hold before I was connected to a very pleasant lady, who was friendly and sympathetic; more important, she acknowledged my sense of urgency. She quickly found time in the schedule when our sick family member could come in—just a few hours later that day. She treated the appointment as a regular office visit, though she did request we come 15 minutes early to complete paperwork. Relieved, we went to see this doctor.

Lessons from the Doctor

An organization has to achieve a balance between the needs of the company and the needs of the customer. Yes, it can be difficult when a business is set up to operate on a certain schedule or relies on certain processes. Yet isn't it amazing how much the customer service experience with these two doctors affected our decision of which one we chose as our family physician? Even before we were "officially" customers, the customer experience mattered significantly.

Aligning with the customer puts the focus squarely on them and their convenience. My experience of looking for a new doctor illustrates a few key points that are relevant for most businesses.

- *Make the process convenient for the customer, not just the company.* Requiring a very sick patient to take a longer (and harder-to-come-by) appointment because that patient is new to your practice is clearly *not* the right thing to do for the customer! In my case, arranging for a follow-up new-patient appointment would have been more beneficial for all concerned, and it probably would have enabled the doctor to see my sick family member sooner. Does your company continue to run business the same old way because "that's how we do things"? Take a hard look at your processes and ask who they really benefit. Some processes have to be in place for regulatory reasons, but when that's not the case, consider revamping any that are not beneficial to the customer experience.

- *Word-of-mouth referrals mean nothing if the customer experience is poor.* Since the first physician I called was a referral from a friend, I trusted that he would be a good doctor. However, the experience we had (long wait on the phone, a surly receptionist, inconvenient appointment) really discouraged us. I found out later that the person who answered the phone was employed by an answering service for all the clinics in this particular physician's network. A nurse from the office called me later in the day to chastise me for not taking the new-patient intake appointment, saying they were very difficult to come by. When I told her I wasn't sure I wanted a doctor who was so busy, she told me all their doctors were very busy. I told her that was fine; we'd find another! Don't count on the fact that your business has frequent referrals or strong online ratings. Treat each interaction as if it counts—because it *does*!

- *You can hear a smile over the phone.* Just by listening to the receptionist at the second doctor's office, I could actually "hear" her smile. She sounded glad to be talking to a potential new patient, and I felt welcome! This is important for anyone representing your company by phone, not only in customer service but also in sales, marketing, and accounts receivable.

- *Think long term, not short.* A patient-doctor relationship can last for many years; once people find a doctor they like, usually they don't go shopping around for a new one unless forced to do so. Making it easy for customers to do business with you helps build trust in the relationship from the beginning. The results may not be immediate, but when the goal is long-term customer relationships, you don't measure only today's campaign ROI, you measure the value of your customers as an important company asset.

What does the experience you provide say to your current and potential customers? Will they come back to you, or will they start looking for the next provider?

Putting Customers First

If your customers are commercial businesses, creating a customer experience that supports their success is even more important. How well do you understand each customer's business? Where might you step in to make that customer's processes easier? A solid knowledge of how to make your customers successful in their business is essential to delivering a customer experience that will make it easier for them to want to keep doing business with you.

Based in Monterrey, Mexico, CEMEX was founded in 1906 and is now one of the world's largest building materials suppliers to both businesses and consumers. CEMEX believes that by focusing on whatever it takes to make its customers more successful will also be good for CEMEX. It tailors its products and services to meet its customers' specific needs by offering integrated solutions geared to a particular vertical industry, rather than always offering separate products. It also studies customers and their business processes to see how they can help improve those processes.

In one case, CEMEX studied contractors who needed supplies of ready-mix concrete and found that when contractors changed their concrete orders at the last minute, it took three hours on average to adjust and deliver those orders. Having seen a 911 call center in Houston operate using GPS to dispatch emergency crews to a situation quickly, CEMEX decided to equip most of its Mexican concrete mixing trucks with GPS technology. This allowed the company to accomplish just-in-time deliveries within a 20-minute window, as opposed to the 3-hour window required by CEMEX's competitors. As a result, CEMEX has been able to better meet the needs of its contractor customers, increase its market share, charge a premium price for expedited delivery service, and reduce costs from unused concrete.[1]

Stepping up and adding value to key parts of the experience is an excellent way to cement trust with your customers, as well as grow your business. It gives the customers the feeling that "we are all in this together," and the favor will most likely be returned to the company through customer loyalty.

DO YOU WANT MY BUSINESS?

Times are tough. Competition is fierce. Customers have high expectations. With all of these factors in play, companies can't afford to treat their customers with anything other than the utmost respect. Ironically, then, considering how some companies treat their customers, it's unclear that they really want their business. If you aren't sure whether your organization is acting as if it wants your customer's business, take a step back and look at its processes from the customer's perspective.

Use these tips to make sure you are ready to follow through on offering a great customer experience:

- *Hire a mystery shopper* to check out all aspects of your customer's buying experience. Notice I didn't say your *sales* experience; again, you need to look at it from the other side of the counter!
- *Talk to customers* who have purchased from you recently. How was their experience? Were their needs met? What could have been better? You might not want to hear all the answers, but if customers aren't happy, they probably won't keep buying from you. Even worse, they could say bad things about you to others.
- *Invite your best customers to come in* and meet with you and your team (or do it via phone conference). Teams get excited when they hear direct positive feedback from customers; you'll also get ideas on what works in your company's customer buying experience and what can be improved.
- *Create customer profiles* of different customer groups and their needs. Make sure your team understands how each "needs group" is unique and how to change the customer approach in each instance.
- *Train your staff* in delivering a "Wow!" customer experience and in relationship-building techniques. Above all, remind them to treat customers as people, not transactions.

Too much to think about? Begin by putting yourself in your customer's shoes, then take one step at a time.

A successful customer experience will become especially important for the next-generation customer who is seeking a new, practical approach to business. These customers want to feel important; they want to feel that they make a difference. Delivering an outstanding customer experience will be essential in extending relationships with them. We can create the best social media sites, connect with our customers on the latest social networks, and even encourage them to spread our message to their friends. However, if they interact with our business and have a poor customer experience, we are putting in jeopardy a relationship that may have already been established in the latest technology channels. It will be those businesses that can create an experience that takes care of the customer, minimizes pain points, and maximizes results for the customer will be talked about positively both online and offline. Are you ready?

Case Study
The Urbane Experience

Urbane Apartments consists of 14 modern, renovated apartment communities in Royal Oak, Michigan, a suburb of Detroit. The company's goal is to inspire enough customer evangelists within the core resident base that the apartments, in a sense, rent themselves through word of mouth (online and offline). Eric Brown, founder of Urbane Apartments, has accomplished this by designing a Resident Experience with high perceived value.

Hunting for an apartment is not usually a fun experience for anyone. It's time-consuming, and the need to find a new place to live can sometimes come up quickly. The process can become even more stressful when relocation to a new city or state is involved. With these issues in mind, Urbane Apartments looked at the customer experience for apartment rentals and realized it begins long before someone moves in. Therefore, the company orchestrated the experience across the resident life cycle, which includes the leasing

(continued)

(*continued*)

experience, the move-in experience, the living experience, and the maintenance experience.

Making Leasing More Fun

Traditionally, leasing an apartment requires days of traipsing through vacant units, with a leasing rep close behind, then reading through mountains of rules and paperwork. Urbane Apartments is making this process more enjoyable by creating an entertaining and relaxing atmosphere for potential residents. Its leasing office, called Urbane Underground, is more like a local coffee house mixed with a disco lounge than a boring office space. The décor is fresh and different, sporting a tropical theme. Well-thought out aromas and music help evoke positive feelings, and the leasing agents spend more time talking about the best local sushi restaurants or their favorite cleaners than the size of the apartments and color of the carpets. Why? Brown's team realizes that the customer already knows these facts through visiting the company's Web site or social media pages, or possibly by having spoken with a current resident.

The Golden Ticket

After prospective residents check in at the leasing office, they are sent off to view units as part of the Urbane "Go Solo" program. Some of the units, which have been lightly staged almost like mini-models, have a Gold Lock on them. Apartment hunters are given a map and a Gold Key that fits any of the vacant units with a Gold Lock. They are welcome to spend time in those units at their leisure and *on their own*; no leasing rep need be present. For up to a week they can go in and out of the units, bring in their significant others, their parents, or their friends and look over the apartments as long as they would like; there's no pressure for a sale. When they are finished looking, they simply drop the key in the mail.

This is quite different from the typical apartment-hunting experience. In fact, Urbane Apartments has been criticized by competitors who say that the Go Solo program is poor customer service.

Potential renters see it differently. They have told Urbane agents that a sales rep usually gets in the way of their touring an apartment. They say they like the way this program allows them time to examine a unit without someone following them around asking awkward sales questions. Urbane's leasing agents are, however, always available to answer questions. (Notably, the number of leases per agent is significantly higher than the industry average.)

A Smooth Move

The most critical time for a new resident is move-in day. For that reason, Urbane Apartments has thought through the steps of this part of the resident life cycle and strives to ensure everything goes smoothly—in advance. Apartments are fully functional, keys have been tested, and support is available for the new residents. Brown gives out his cell phone number to each new resident in case of any problems. He wants to be fully available to his residents; he does not hide behind voicemail. Additionally, if a current resident later wants to move to another Urbane property, an agent will make it easier by providing moving trucks for free.

The Urbane Life

The longest part of the resident life cycle is the living experience, and Urbane Apartments strives to make daily life wonderful for its residents. For example, its "Urbane Loves Pets" program has no size or breed restrictions, and no additional pet fees are imposed—a major plus for a pet owner. And by focusing its energies on leasing to highly qualified prospects, Urbane Apartments finds that not only do they get responsible and conscientious residents, those residents also usually have well-behaved pets.

Urbane Apartments also works to connect with its residents online. It publishes a blog called "The Urbane Life," where the company shares posts about topics that are relevant to residents, such as local restaurants, music events, and even pets. Its online community is a place where residents can get to know each other and offer their feedback to Urbane management.

(continued)

(*continued*)

Urbane hosts regular social activities for its residents as well; these are usually held off-site and in partnership with local businesses. The events are well attended and generate buzz through the social media chatter of residents and their friends who come by. Brown also decided to reinvent the community's seldom-used clubhouses; he now offers them as free coworking spaces for residents and other members of the community. On some days, 3 to 4 people can be found using them; other days, 15 to 18 people. Most days, busy consultants and entrepreneurs can be found using the coworking spaces and sharing on their social networks where they are and what they are doing (all hosted by Brown and his team).

Keeping It Up

Brown and his team strive to make all the various touch point exchanges with residents go as smoothly as possible. For example, many of the firm's apartments are of a 1960s vintage, and while all have been modernized and updated, things still do break down. Thus, ongoing maintenance interactions are often where "the rubber meets the road." Brown's team works to set expectations clearly. If there is an emergency repair needed, it gets fixed right away. Other issues may take a little longer; for these, Urbane Apartments provides a time estimate and then keeps its commitments. Per Brown, "If things go badly, we want to reach out and fix it. We need to listen to our customers and their concerns, since many times what they are upset about isn't the real issue. If we just listen to them, and when they are finished we talk about it rationally with them, this conversation can be a hidden gem for us. We can turn angry residents into lifelong evangelists."

Understanding Resident Needs

Listening to residents has improved the quality of life at Urbane Apartments, and it has given the company fantastic ideas on how to create a resident experience that rocks. For example, as a result of resident feedback, Urbane developed an online system that residents can use to pay their rent, as well as submit service requests. A survey is also included as part of the online system. Brown and his team use it to ask about resident satisfaction across all four areas of the resident life cycle (leasing, move-in, living, and maintenance). As another example, Urbane Apartments started using Google Voice on its phones to better enable staff to track incoming calls. They discovered that if they could stay open an additional two hours a day, they would be able to capture 99 percent of previously missed calls, allowing them to better address service issues and arrange for package pickups. The Urbane Apartments leasing center is now open from 8:00 AM to 9:00 PM weekdays (none of its competitors are open after 6:00 PM). This alone has resulted in an uptick in occupancy rates.

Results

Urbane Apartments regularly looks for ways to enhance the resident experience. The majority of its marketing outreach has nothing to do with renting apartments. In fact, the company has transitioned most of its marketing budget inward, focusing on its existing residents and helping them lead a better lifestyle by meeting their needs to interact with their friends and enjoy living in Royal Oak.

Only good things have happened since Urbane Apartments has increased its focus on the customer. Resident retention has significantly improved. Residents have spread the word through their own tight-knit online and offline social networks about the great place where they live. As a result, Urbane Apartments has consistently shown 98 to 100 percent occupancy across its portfolio, in spite of the difficult economy in the Detroit metropolitan area. Brown says, "We want to do what's right for our residents. We listen for processes that don't work for them then reinvent the experience."

Lessons

Brown encourages others to take a hard look at their customer experience. Is it delivering what you *think* it is? Is it what the customer really wants? Likewise, take a hard look at your own internal

(*continued*)

(continued)

processes. Just because your processes are the same ones being used by others in the industry doesn't mean they are beneficial for your customer. Keep the processes that are really necessary for successfully running the business, make sure to meet the customer's needs, and orchestrate an experience that works for your business *and* for your customer.

Information taken from a personal interview with Eric Brown on January 7, 2011.

R
O
C—CUSTOMER-FOCUSED CULTURE
K

It all starts here.

Culture: "The attitudes, feelings, values, and behaviors that characterize and inform society as a whole or any social group within it."[1]

If you have a business, you have a company culture—regardless of the size of your organization. Applying the definition above, business culture is a set of values and beliefs that convey what your company represents. They provide a sense of identity for employees, customers, and suppliers, as well as the public. The beliefs and values of a company's people compose the core of its culture;[2] its leaders bring this value system to life and make it real.

The company culture is an important part of what motivates employees to work for and stay with a business. Managers must nurture it if they want to create a great employee experience—which correlates directly with a great customer experience.

Unfortunately, many companies pay lip service to being "customer-centric" but do little to support that strategy. A strong customer-focused culture starts with a customer-focused leader (often an executive, founder, or CEO) who is able to instill passion and loyalty in employees, inspire other business leaders to serve employees as well as the company, open communications within the company, and measure and reward people in ways that will motivate them to continue to serve clients and protect the culture. When done well, a true customer-focused culture can be a competitive differentiator, one that is very difficult for others to replicate.

Chapter 9

CULTURE OF CUSTOMER SERVICE

The companies profiled in the case studies in this book all have one quality in common: a customer-service culture. And all of the customer-focused leaders I interviewed for these studies shared similar approaches with me, whether they head a large company or a small business. These can be distilled into the following guidelines:

- *Listen to customers* to understand their needs.
- *Initiate a customer feedback process* (formal or informal) and use what you learn from it to take action and make changes.
- *Think through the customer experience* and work with customer-facing employees to serve customers well at each touch point.
- *Assemble a clear set of values* focused around employee and customer success, along with a great employee experience.
- *Have a sense of urgency, and care for every customer* throughout the organization—from founder or president to customer-facing staff to behind-the-scenes employees.
- *Interact with employees continuously* about what service looks like and what their customers need.
- *Make customer service part of the company DNA,* which means look for it in the people you hire, your suppliers and partners, and your management team—who should lead by serving.

PUT PEOPLE FIRST

The value an organization puts on customer service says a lot about that company. From the perspective of customers, how they're treated reveals the true focus of an organization. How does your company prioritize customers and their needs? Do you try to get them off the phone quickly so you can go on to other calls? Or do you take the time to follow a problem through to its resolution, while taking ownership for it? Do customers have to repeat their information multiple times as they interact with you? Or do you use the information you have already gathered, recorded, and maintained about them to make your time together more effective (a benefit for both parties)?

From the employee perspective, how customers are served demonstrates whether or not the organization treats all people with respect. This is especially important for contact center and customer service employees, who are sometimes treated as just another "warm body in a seat." Are they instructed to reply from a set of scripted responses, or are staff members free to answer the customer's question in their own words? Are they required to follow company policy—even if it's not what's right for the customer or situation, or are they empowered to resolve the customer's problem?

Set the Stage

An organization's culture sets its tone and reinforces its values. At the most admired customer-focused organizations, the leadership recognizes that customer service isn't a department; it's a companywide focus. It's everyone's job. This is most apparent when customer service is an integral part of the corporate culture.

Marriott International, for example, conveys a strong service culture that encourages an emotional tie between the company and its associates. The evidence can be seen in the kind of service Marriott associates provide their customers. The hotel chain hires people who have the passion to serve and make guests so comfortable so they want to come back. Marriott's associates go above and beyond for their guests.

A story I read on Mr. Bill Marriott's blog, "Marriott on the Move," shares how one associate gave a guest the shirt off his back—well, actually, the pants off his legs! The Marriott guest had accidentally packed his wife's black slacks in his suitcase instead of his own, and he discovered the mix-up only a short time before he had to leave for a business meeting. Frantic, he went to the front desk hoping there might be a spare pair of slacks in the lost and found, or, failing that, he wanted directions to a nearby store where he could buy a pair. With only minutes to spare before the meeting and no pants to be found, the Marriott associate realized he wore the same size as the guest and offered the guest the very slacks he was wearing. They were, indeed, a perfect fit; the guest made it to his meeting on time, and the associate changed into a pair of casual pants he had brought with him to work.

But that's not the end of the story.

This blog post also had comments from guests at other Marriott properties who likewise were thrilled by the customer service they had received from the hotel's associates—emphasizing that this kind of customer service is truly ingrained throughout the Marriott culture.[1]

Another example of a strong customer-focused culture can be found at Nordstrom department stores. In addition to its legendary customer service, Nordstrom is committed to the people aspect of its business at all customer touch points. This is apparent even in the chain's off-price division, Nordstrom Rack. These stores offer a wide selection of apparel, accessories, and shoes from Nordstrom stores and Nordstrom.com at reduced prices, as well as special-value items purchased just for Nordstrom Rack. Most clearance-type stores are not usually places where shoppers expect to receive attentive customer service. But Nordstrom's strong culture of customer service carries over unmistakably to Nordstrom Rack, made clear in the following excerpt from a Nordstrom Rack job listing. Notice the customer focus in each position description (emphasis mine).[2]

We are currently looking for individuals with a positive and energetic attitude who are interested in Sales, Stock, or Customer Service positions. Key Responsibilities:

- Sales people provide great service through positive interactions and product knowledge with *each and every customer.*
- Customer Service Representatives *meet our customers' expectations* with professional, efficient service at the point of sale.
- Stock people *support our customers* by keeping our fixtures full with merchandise that is accurately ticketed.

Every position listed is tied back to its impact on the customer. It's all about *people.*

I experienced this focus on the customer for myself when I was shopping at the local Nordstrom Rack. While I was busy searching for a new pair of shoes (Nordstrom's original product), my two sons went looking for a tie for a special occasion. When I went over to check on them, I found one of the store employees was not only showing my boys some ties, she was giving them a lesson in how to tie them. She was cheerful, friendly, and very patient, even when they got it wrong. She then went in the back and found a sheet of instructions describing the steps involved in tying a tie—"In case you forget how," she told my sons. I was surprised and pleased at the interest she took in making sure these two young men learned to tie their ties properly. In the process, she not only made a sale, she may have made two more lifetime Nordstrom customers.

When customer service is integral to a company's culture, it comes across in everything it does. Employees make each decision with the customer in mind. New staff is hired based on their ability to be passionate about people. Each employee treats every colleague, customer, and vendor with respect. The actions and attitudes of company leaders become models for what it looks like to serve others. Customer service truly becomes part of a company's DNA.

WHAT WE VALUE

It's not enough, however, to establish a customer-service culture. Many organizations start out with good intentions in this area but for various reasons lose their way as they grow, hit difficult circumstances, or change leadership.

Recall the success guidelines listed at the beginning of this chapter; the one that helps to keep the culture fires burning is to "assemble a clear set of company values." Organizations that maintain a clear focus on company values have made a commitment to live and breathe those values, day in and day out. The story of one such company started fairly simply: with two young engineers working out of a garage.

The HP Way

My first job out of college was with Hewlett-Packard, now known simply as HP. It was an organization where clear values were instilled in all of us by the founders, Bill Hewlett and Dave Packard, who could be seen on a regular basis wandering the halls and talking to employees about what we were doing. The company's values were embodied in the "HP Way," a management philosophy centered on integrity, respect for individuals, teamwork, innovation, and contribution to customers and the community. Managers shared this approach with all employees, and while it wasn't something that we memorized or carried around on cards, we were all trained to recognize and live it as the HP way of doing business.

Shortly before David Packard passed away, in 1996, he wrote a book called *The HP Way* and gave a copy to all of us employees. Here's what he wrote inside the front cover:[3]

> To all HP People:
>
> I hope you'll enjoy this account of how Bill and I started the company and how it developed into a worldwide leader in technology, innovation and business enterprise. I have also described those HP values and management principles that together have become known as the "HP Way."
>
> HP's success is due to the talents and dedication of you and your colleagues and of the people who have gone before you. Together we have built a company without peer, and I hope, as you read the pages that follow, you will feel a deep sense of pride and satisfaction in what we have accomplished.
>
> Sincerely,
> Dave

Bill and Dave were very clear about the company values; they never wavered on the company's ultimate goal. Many of us who worked there at that time not only look back on those days with fond memories, we've also taken those business philosophies forward with us to other companies.

The Culture Is the Brand

Another inspirational company with a strong customer service culture is online retailer Zappos.com. Early in the company's history, CEO Tony Hsieh wanted to establish a culture for employees in order to keep them committed to the culture already under development. Based on employee discussions, Hsieh and his team decided to develop a Culture Book; they asked all employees to share their thoughts about the company's culture. In an attempt to ensure that each person's authentic voice was heard, the team printed the employees' own words; they didn't edit the entries. They wanted to document the truth about the Zappos.com culture (both good and bad).

The first Culture Book was produced in 2004, and a new version is published each year. The book still shares the unedited voices of the company's employees and now also includes the perspective of partners, vendors, and even customers. It's free and available to all employees and the general public.

As Hsieh describes in his own book, *Delivering Happiness: A Path to Profits, Passion, and Purpose,* it was suggested that the team come up with a list of attributes they were looking for in new hires, to aid in bringing in people who were the right fit for the Zappos.com culture. To compile this list, Hsieh gathered input from all employees; from an initial list of 37 core values, 10 were identified as most important. Here they are:

Zappos Core Values[4]
1. Deliver WOW Through Service.
2. Embrace and Drive Change.
3. Create Fun and a Little Weirdness.
4. Be Adventurous, Creative, and Open-Minded.
5. Pursue Growth and Learning.
6. Build Open and Honest Relationships with Communication.
7. Build a Positive Team and Family Spirit.
8. Do More with Less.
9. Be Passionate and Determined.
10. Be Humble.

These core values are not just something impressive to put on a poster and hang on the wall. Interview questions that correspond to each of the core values are asked of all job candidates, and, as Hsieh explains in his book, new employees have to "sign that they have read the core values document and understand that living up to the core values is part of their job expectation." Zappos.com believes strongly in protecting its company culture. Hsieh wrote, "we were committed to living up to our core values in everything we did, not just referring to them when it was convenient." Zappos.com continues to live by them today.

According to a personal interview with Maura Sullivan, senior manager on the Zappos Customer Loyalty Team, the Zappos Core Values help employees feel empowered to provide amazing service to their customers. She shared a story of one customer service representative who received an e-mail from a deployed member of the U.S. military. At that time, Zappos was selling electronics, and the e-mail indicated that an Xbox had been sent to this customer instead of the clothing he had ordered. He wanted to know how to return it. The Zappos rep made the decision to let him keep the Xbox as a thank-you for serving our country, then also sent him what he had originally ordered. Word got out about this rep's initiative, and the rep's colleagues decided to do even more: assemble a care package for the soldier and his buddies. They collected fun items and old Xbox games, then they shipped them overseas to the soldier. To show his appreciation to Zappos, the soldier sent back photos of himself and the other soldiers playing Xbox on their breaks.

Sullivan explained that because Zappos's hiring practices are so tightly linked to the company's core values, managers know they are selecting employees who have a natural affinity with the core values. As a result, each employee feels responsible for keeping the Zappos culture strong. "The attitude is that it is not up to me to preserve the culture; it is up to everybody," says Sullivan.

When a company has a strong corporate culture, all employees know its values; they can verbalize them because they have internalized them, and they live by them on a daily basis. Some organizations give their employees a card imprinted with the corporate values to carry with them; others ask employees annually to determine one way they can change what they are doing to better support the values. This helps employees stay excited about the company and guides their daily decision making.

KEEP IT GOING

A company can't just create a customer service culture, outline company values, and consider the work to be finished. Sustaining this type of culture is a journey, not a destination, and the path can take a number of turns. To that end, some larger corporations have established a chief customer officer (CCO) position. This role can work well for companies that are ready to have a senior executive take the responsibility for driving the effort to get closer to the customer. The person in this position should be a leader who can help bring the voice of the customer into the company, drive initiatives and alignment across departments, champion clear metrics for measuring progress, and be empowered to work as a peer on the senior management team. (A valuable resource for determining whether your corporation is ready for a CCO is *Chief Customer Officer: Getting Past Lip Service to Passionate Action*, by Jeanne Bliss.[5])

Leaders of small to midsized businesses and those companies not yet ready for a CCO can help strengthen the culture through close involvement of the leadership team with their customers. Citibank's Senior Vice President of Social Media, Frank Eliason, is in favor of the CCO role but suggests that regardless of whether an organization puts one in place, all of a company's leaders should stay close to customers in order to help engender the culture of customer service. Eliason recommends executives achieve this by engaging in regular customer contact and actively listening to customers and their feedback. As discussed in Chapter 1, if your customers are active in social media, search those channels for mentions of your company or industry to gain direct access to information about your brand or products. This effort can complement a formal or informal customer feedback (VOC) program.

Pursue the Truth

Additionally, it is important to spend time talking with customer-facing teams. According to Eliason, "Senior management should be prepared; there will be a lot of 'smoke and mirrors' since employees want to look good in front of their leaders. They need to be given permission to show the bad and the ugly along with the good; they need to be able to share the reality of what is happening on the front lines with customers."

People in positions of leadership often believe they already have a customer service culture. They are frequently proven wrong, however, when they ask customers directly about their experiences. "The challenge is that employees filter what goes up the chain and don't readily share the truth upward. That's why TV shows like *Undercover Boss* are so exciting," Eliason said in a personal interview. The show allows CEOs to see their companies from the perspective of the employees. It is inspiring to watch the lightbulb turn on when these leaders of large corporations are exposed to the honest truth about what goes on at the front lines.

It is important for companies of all sizes to create a culture of customer service, one that spans across every level and reaches each individual in the company. Management teams, from middle management to the founder or CEO, all need to be actively involved in modeling the values of the culture, training and coaching their employees on behaviors that support it, and keeping policies simple so that they unobtrusively enhance a remarkable customer experience.

As the business grows, the culture and values will become critical components in bringing in new people who can also become believers and rally behind the cause of the customer. By working together, the entire organization will be able to sustain the passion necessary to offer great experiences for both customers and employees.

Chapter 10

MEASURE WHAT MATTERS

Metrics are becoming a vital part of doing business these days. In the past, some companies operated in a very passive and intuitive way, whereas today companies are much more metrics-driven as they strive to define their business progress in measurable terms. Customer-focused organizations measure their organizations in such a way that enables them to bring the whole business together around a common goal: growing the company through their customers. These organizations know the importance of understanding which programs are making an impact on business goals, as well as on customer relationships. They also recognize the need to measure success indications from the customer perspective. These include customer retention, customer loyalty, and evangelism—followed by increased revenues.

To achieve success in these areas, companies need to be able to measure how well they are handling the customer experience, as well as how they are performing against customer expectations. They need metrics that tell them what's happening during customer interactions, how customers feel about those interactions with the company, and what customers do as a result of their experiences.

Usually, there is no lack of data of this sort at most organizations. Rather, what's missing is the ability to use that data to gain insights that make a difference—or, as some would say, "move the needle" for the business. Good analytics can help produce actionable insights, and relevant metrics will measure the outcomes and reveal areas that need attention. When the results are measured and shared across the company, and everyone is held accountable, everyone wins—company and customer.

CUSTOMER-FOCUSED METRICS

In the same way a mother uses a measuring stick to track how tall her children are growing, companies use metrics to track how well they are performing. There are many types of business metrics; customer-focused metrics should be based on what is valuable to customers—and be measured from their perspective. Metrics such as impressions, leads, or number of social media followers tend to be used in marketing, whereas metrics such as call handle times and queue lengths are used in contact centers. These metrics evaluate activities from a company perspective. In contrast, metrics such as "percentage of information relevant to my needs" or "time taken to resolve a problem" gauge success from a customer's perspective.

When I worked at HP, we asked ourselves the following question to determine the success of customer experience initiatives: Does what we are doing show from the customer's perspective? It's important to link what is most important to a customer back to the business goals and track these elements accordingly.

What's the Goal?

Some companies maintain huge dashboards covered with charts and graphs that dazzle the eyes. It can be a superhuman feat to stay on top of all of those metrics—much less act upon them. Often the organizations that obtain the best results are those that focus on a few key measures that make an impact on what really matters.

The metrics that companies choose to track the components of their customer strategy will vary greatly depending on each company's specific goals. According to Esteban Kolsky, an expert on customer strategy and principal and founder of ThinkJar LLC, no single metric works for everybody. Instead, it is more important to look at what a business is trying to accomplish before determining which metrics to track.

For example, if a company wants to focus on improving customer service, it needs to examine why it wants to do that. Is it being demanded of the company, or does it see it as a core differentiator? If the company hopes to get closer to customers, what is the purpose: to keep up with the latest trend, or to grow the business? Kolsky advocates the importance of identifying a strategic measurement model and monitoring across the right metrics, connected to specific business goals, in order to truly see the impact.

For example, according to Kolsky, if the goal is to improve customer loyalty, it is not enough just to measure whether loyalty improved. The business should also measure whether revenues increased and whether there was an uptick in the number of returning customers year-on-year. Kolsky also believes it is important to tie the measures to the right goals in order to see if there has truly been a measurable impact. This is done by gauging success across the entire business, rather than within only one function or area. All parts of the organization must come together and link back to business success.

A strong measurement program will include metrics that can measure impact to the business at the micro level (the front line) in near-real time, as well as show business impact at the macro level (for the company executives to track). These measurements also need to assess both efficiency (how well operations are running) and effectiveness (how well we provide the right customer information to the right employees at the right time) in order to help a business truly meet its goals.[1]

MOVE FROM DATA TO INSIGHT TO ACTION

Metrics can help a business evaluate its bottom-line success and reveal areas of potential concern, but it is the right data and keen insights that drive real change.

Metrics have to tell a story. Gone are the days when a few charts and reports were all that were required. To demonstrate impact, we need to help everyone in our organization understand *why* we are focused on these areas and *how* they make a difference to the company. Telling senior management that "customer engagement scores have increased for the past eight quarters" is somewhat interesting, but telling senior management that "in this same time period, quarterly sales increased 8 percent, on average, and a steady decline in customer attrition of

24 percent has been associated with increased customer engagement" really starts to tell a story.[2]

This may require a new way of thinking for market research teams that aren't used to sharing this type of information. According to Chris Cottle, Executive VP of Marketing and Products at Allegiance, Inc., a leading provider of Voice-of-the-Customer (VOC) solutions, successful VOC programs have strong leaders who can deliver a business story around the reasons behind a customer-centric focus. It's not enough to prove a program is effective; it's equally important that others buy into it.

The best approach is to focus on a few key metrics that support business goals, then use our customer feedback data and analytics to help provide actionable insight. According to Cottle, companies already collect a large amount of data; however, many don't always do anything with it. "We should be looking for more insight from the data we already have, not looking for more data." he asserts.

So how do we put a process in place to measure the success of our customer strategy and tell a compelling story? A high-level process could look like the following:

1. Gather feedback from customers through a formal or informal VOC program.
2. Pair that feedback with other data the company already has on customers. This could include survey data (*transactional*, which would take place based on a specific interaction, and *relational*, which would be delivered at set times during the year to determine how customers are feeling about their overall relationship with the business), as well as unsolicited feedback from social media, Web site feedback forms, or information shared with a sales rep or customer service employee.
3. Analyze the feedback and data to gain insight into that customer or group of customers, their value to the company, their needs and preferences, and their predicted behaviors.
4. Determine what actions the company can take to improve the customer experience based on the analysis.
5. Share the appropriate information with each touch point that impacts the customer, ensuring that these points of contact have what they need to take action and better serve customers.

Analytics Play a Role

Keeping the right outcomes in mind, companies can implement the appropriate analytics to uncover the kind of customer insights that will help drive decisions. Cottle shares five levels of analytics, along with the insight that each uncovers:

1. *Data:* The raw information from customer feedback systems
2. *Charts:* Visual representation of the data
3. *Reports:* Data analysis that's often targeted for a specific audience
4. *Prescriptive Analytics:* Suggestions on changes or improvements to make based on data and its context
5. *Predictive Analytics:* Potential outcomes for the business determined from the data and its context (e.g., if we do *x*, we will get *y*)

Cottle maintains that although these last two levels are harder to achieve, an employee with a passion for analytics can use an analytics package or program to produce key insights, which can then be used to drive action in a company.

The benefits of utilizing a cohesive feedback, analytics, and metrics system that links results back to business goals come from *taking action* on the suggested and predicted insights. Companies that put this type of system in place, along with a similar system for employee feedback and metrics, are typically able to reap such benefits as lower costs, improved resource allocations, reduced churn or risk, enhanced marketing effectiveness, improved share of wallet, and increased positive referrals.[3]

SATISFACTION: DOES IT MATTER?

Many companies cite "having satisfied customers" as their main goal in a customer-focused initiative. Customer satisfaction is only the entry point, however, and it's not a strong entry point. What does "satisfaction" really mean to a customer? For some customers, it might mean that they received everything they purchased, the way they wanted it, so they could go about their business. Other customers may not be satisfied until they feel that the company has gone "above and beyond" for them. There are even companies that push their customers to state that they are "completely satisfied" with a transaction or experience even if they are not.

For example, I was in and out of the local office of a nationally known car rental company several times last summer while the air conditioning in my car was being repaired. Each time I returned a car, I was asked whether I was "completely satisfied" with my experience. My response to this question varied, depending on which car I had been given, how clean the car was, and how long I had to wait to return it. The one time I was given an upgraded car, I *definitely* felt completely satisfied! Overall, though, I also felt pressured by the company's employees to always rate them tops in satisfaction. Had I done so, what good would it have done the company, since my feedback wouldn't have been an indication of true satisfaction on my part?

Are You Really Satisfied?

Satisfaction is driven by a variety of factors. Rather than just asking your customers if they are satisfied, it is more valuable to try and understand what exactly makes them feel that way. This could be as simple as asking them to share what they liked or didn't like about their transaction or experience. Needless to say, when companies ask these more pointed questions, they have to be prepared to listen to the ranting of disgruntled customers. It is necessary not only to get the information but also to act on it. Action should be both immediate (fix this issue) and long term (how can we avoid this problem in the future?).

What about a customer who is being held "hostage" by a company— by which I mean those who have no other options for a specific service. For example, only one package delivery company serves a remote area or the company you work for is locked in a contract with a certain service provider. Does customer satisfaction in these cases lead to long-term loyalty, or would customers jump ship when other options become available?

Beyond Satisfaction

For a number of reasons, customers defect even when they claim on surveys to be satisfied with a company, product, or service. By its nature, customer satisfaction is a backward-looking metric, so it doesn't tell a business the whole story; it can only indicate how pleased, or not, a customer was with a single transaction. Nor does satisfaction predict the strength of a customer relationship or the opportunity for future business. When assessing the customer satisfaction metric, then, it should be used as only one measure of customer loyalty. Both the context and the drivers also need to be reviewed during the assessment.

Remember, customer satisfaction is only the entry point. Nurturing loyal customers who will purchase from you repeatedly, buy more, and recommend your business to others requires attention to customers beyond their "satisfaction level."

One method of going beyond satisfaction metrics is the Net Promoter approach. Net Promoter is both a metric (Net Promoter Score, or NPS), as well as a discipline, to drive improvements in customer loyalty and business growth. It is based on asking customers how likely they would be to recommend your business to a friend. Those customers who answer this question with a strongly positive likelihood are considered Promoters; these are a company's loyalists. Those customers who answer this question with a strongly negative likelihood are considered Detractors; these are disgruntled customers who could spread negative impressions about your company. Those in-between are the Passives; they could be swayed either way, depending on the customer experience.

The NPS is calculated by subtracting the percentage of Detractors from the percentage of Promoters. Many companies use NPS to help them track the success of their customer programs—are they creating more Promoters and reducing the number of Detractors? These companies look at how each interaction with a company can potentially affect customers and tune their customer experience accordingly.[4]

MEASURING CUSTOMER PERCEPTION

Metrics geared to the customer relationship can begin to provide a deeper level of insight into how the customer feels about the company. Measuring what matters to customers is one of the best ways to ensure that a company can begin to predict business results. Janet LeBlanc, president of Janet LeBlanc + Associates, a leading authority in the area of customer value and experience management, recommends that companies understand and manage the value that customers perceive in a company's products and services.

LeBlanc explains that customer value is a good measure of what matters to customers and consists of two factors: *quality* and *price*. Quality is defined best by the customer, based on what he or she values most about the customer experience. Price is the second factor, and customers evaluate it by asking themselves whether the product or service is worth what they paid for it.

Although customer perceptions of quality and price (i.e., value) are not always factored into the previously discussed satisfaction and loyalty metrics, according to LeBlanc, in her years of business experience, customer value has been found to be one of the best predictors of business success.

Five Pillars

LeBlanc advocates launching a Customer Value Management Program in order to first understand and then take action on customer value perceptions. This goes back to the fundamentals of a customer experience management program. Gather data on what customers value most, use these priorities to incorporate customer experience improvements throughout the organization, and reinforce to all employees that the overriding objective is to delight the customer. LeBlanc evaluates the various aspects of an end-to-end customer experience based on five pillars as follows:

1. *Product offering:* The product or service features and benefits a company is offering.
2. *Product delivery or execution:* Whether the product or service performs as expected.
3. *Price:* Whether the product or service was worth the price.
4. *Service culture:* The culture a business promises, and whether it delivers on this.
5. *Reputation/image:* The impact a brand image has on the perception of quality and value for a customer.

For a business to understand how the customer perceives the value it offers, both the five pillars and the actual customer experience touch points need to be assessed. By conducting detailed statistical analysis on the results, a business can determine which parts of its customer experience are having the greatest impact on customer perceptions of value—and on the possibility that customers will return to buy again.

Customer perceptions can be found through surveys conducted with both customers and noncustomers. LeBlanc prefers a 10-point (rather than the more traditional 5-point) performance scale—from very delighted to very unhappy—to give customers more opportunity to reveal the nuances in their perceptions. She also points out the importance of using statistical analysis to derive customer priorities. Most surveys ask customers to rate, or rank-order, those areas of the experience that are most important to them; however, customers usually end up rating everything as important (they assume it must be so, since it was included in the survey). Customers can't always distinguish which areas have the greatest impact. By using Customer Value Analysis techniques, whereby priorities are mathematically derived, LeBlanc has seen results that are more precise in determining customer importance.

Making It Work

While the Customer Value Management Program is a solid approach to understanding customers, it is a process that may take several business periods in order to produce statistically significant results. Per LeBlanc, in the short term it is possible to measure and monitor the overall customer perception of value through customer surveys. Survey results should then be shared with all employees within an organization (not just those in customer service) in a way that makes it relevant to their roles. "When a manager or supervisor links customer needs to an employee's specific strengths or weaknesses, the result is an individual action plan for that employee to improve and build on [his or her] strengths," says LeBlanc. She also explains that promoting customer success stories is an effective way to keep employees engaged in the process: "Here is what the customer told us; these employees made these changes, and this is what we saw as a result." Consequently, employees will see a real connection between their roles and business success. They will believe in the program and have greater confidence that they are making a difference. In the end, employees will continue to be motivated to do a great job for the customer.[5]

NEW METRICS FOR MEASURING THE CUSTOMER SERVICE EXPERIENCE

Social media has brought the need to provide outstanding customer service back to the forefront of business strategy. Business customers as well as consumers have mobile devices right at their fingertips, which allow them to interact with their social networks on a regular basis. Today, when something goes wrong from the customer perspective, they not only get mad, they go straight to Twitter, Facebook, and other social media sites to vent their frustrations.

> I have been waiting on the phone for my sales rep for 15 minutes! Come on, Company XYZ, are you there?

Or,

> I attended a concert at ABC Amphitheater last night, and the sound was terrible. I'm never going back there. Fail.

What does this mean for companies, large and small? It means the public practice of customer service has become a business imperative. Customer service successes, as well as failures, are easily visible to customers and competitors alike. As a result, the metrics being used today to measure the results of traditional customer service interactions are not entirely adequate to capture this "new world." Some rethinking is required. That's not to say we should abandon existing metrics, only that businesses have to figure out how to incorporate ways of measuring new, digital interactions in order to understand the success (or failure) of their customer service processes.

To adjust to this shift, we need to keep in mind the customer expectations of a service experience. Customers are looking for companies to do the following:

- *Be fast:* Get back to me and respond quickly.
- *Be accurate:* Get me the right answer; solve my problem.
- *Be friendly:* I am already feeling inconvenienced; don't make it worse!

A Twist on Traditional Metrics

The traditional customer-focused service metrics—time to respond, first contact resolution, time to resolve, customer satisfaction, customer loyalty, and so on—are still important to measure and track in this new world. However, some of these metrics will be greatly affected by the widespread use of social media. (*Note:* If your organization is still focused solely on efficiency metrics, such as call handle time, rather than on tracking some of the previously mentioned metrics, it's time to make a dramatic shift in order to accurately measure the customer experience your company offers.)

Let's review how some of the traditional customer service metrics have been impacted by customer interactions taking place in social media channels.

Time to Respond

When customers use real-time social media tools, response time becomes a critical measure. Many customers are using social media as an escalation path, so their expectations are high. What is acceptable in terms of time to respond via e-mail, for example, will not suffice in social media channels. So, while the metric remains the same (response time), the service levels and accepted results are different. As soon as a company sees a customer escalation in social media regarding a service or product complaint, it needs to respond quickly and get any problem resolved, ASAP. (Keep in mind that in order for this to be successful, it is also important for the company to clearly define the criteria for what a social media escalation looks like.)

First Contact Resolution and Time to Resolve

These are still important metrics for customer service interactions via social media. That said, the first contact resolution metric may also need to be revised slightly. For example, say a customer complains about an issue with your company via Twitter, but Twitter allows only 140 characters per Tweet; so if the issue is at all complex, a single Tweet probably won't be sufficient to describe it. The point is, many times, customer service issues can't be completely resolved via social media channels; they need to be followed up via phone or e-mail. In these cases, the first contact resolution metric may need to be adjusted to incorporate multiple touch points.

In other words, the social media tool is often just the gateway to the service interaction; once a customer is brought back into traditional assisted support channels (e.g., e-mail or phone), the more traditional customer service metrics can be applied.

Keep in mind that issues raised via social media may need to be resolved faster than was previously required, because now the world is watching—and waiting.

Other Metrics for Social Media Customer Service

Customers today will not hesitate to talk about your customer service response, or lack thereof, via social media. To understand and track these conversations, it is important to monitor some of the following metrics:

- *Sentiment:* Customer emotions can be a bit tricky to interpret via an electronic medium, yet they are a key factor in ascertaining customer satisfaction levels in social media. What are the sentiments being expressed in the Tweets, Facebook updates, blog postings, and community forum threads regarding your products or services? Positive? Negative? Trending one way or the other?

- *Number of issues coming in versus number resolved:* Many customer issues raised in social media channels such as Twitter, Facebook, blogs, or community forums *can* be resolved to the customer's satisfaction. There will also be a number that cannot. What makes the difference? Based on my experience, I've found that sometimes customers just want to be heard. They don't want you to do anything about it; they just want others to acknowledge their concern. In these cases, the company should let its customers know it is available to assist them, if desired. It's a good idea to track these types of issues, including how many have been resolved, so that the number of people who are complaining for the sake of complaining can be monitored over time.

- *Frequency:* Another area to track is how frequently customer service issues are raised in social media channels. This metric can be an indicator of a widespread problem, a shift in customer interaction preference, or a breakdown in other company service channels. Measuring volumes and frequencies will also enable you to more accurately determine staffing requirements needed to handle social media customer service (don't forget the weekends!).

- *Friendliness:* Like sentiment, this is a qualitative measure. How do company reps come across in their customer service responses via social media? Customers likely expect customer service employees who staff these sites to be more outgoing, less formal, and easier to talk with than traditional contact center reps.
- *Call deflections:* Track this metric in social media channels such as online peer-to-peer support communities, along with other self-service paths. Keep in mind, however, that social media sites are often used as escalation paths, so this metric may be skewed, as customers may have already tried to call.

Finally, customer satisfaction and loyalty should continue to be measured across the customer experience, including social media touch points. In fact, satisfaction levels of customers interacting via social media may be even more critical, in that some of these people may have a large sphere of online influence, and all of these interactions are very public.[6]

MEASURING THE SUCCESS OF CUSTOMER STRATEGY

So far in this chapter, we have looked at several aspects of measuring the success of a customer strategy. At a minimum, it is important to monitor how the answers to the following questions are affecting the success of your company's customer strategy:

- *How many customers did we keep from last year?* Do you know? Many businesses find that they are good at tracking new customers but lose sight of those who "slip out the back."
- *If we lost customers, why?* Ideally, you will conduct this analysis each time you lose a customer—reach out immediately and find out what went wrong. By doing this religiously, you may be able to salvage some of these valuable relationships.
- *Why do our best customers keep doing business with us?* Ask them! Find out whether it's your offerings, your service, your people, or all of the above. It will help to prioritize where to focus your improvements, as well as to identify what to keep on doing. It may also highlight potential areas of concern for certain clients.

- *How many of our loyal customers can help us sell more?* Existing customers can do this for us in many ways: buying additional products or services themselves, referring our company to others, and sharing testimonials about their great customer experiences. When is the last time you asked a customer for a testimonial? Make doing so a regular part of doing business!

Treating the Customer as an Asset

Incredibly, many companies today still measure their customer service teams based on how many calls or online chats they process in an hour. As a result, customer service representatives try to get customers off the phone or online chat as soon as possible in order to move on so they can "make their numbers." Often, the end result is that customers have to call again to finish their transactions, whether to get a question answered or a problem resolved. These types of metrics are employed when organizations regard the customer service team as a cost center rather than as a valuable touch point.

I was once a member of a team of consultants where our client was a large company with multiple call centers; each was managed out of a different organization. In the process of mapping out the customer experience, I sat with some of the customer service phone reps to learn more about what customers had to go through to accomplish their tasks with this organization. My visit to the first call center on the list left me feeling very stressed out. It was clear to me the phone agent I shadowed was being measured on how quickly she could get customers off the phone. She talked fast, barely listened to what each customer was asking, and was even a bit rude. She did process quite a few calls in that hour; however, I am not sure that her customers were satisfied with the results. Likely, many had to call back to complete their transactions as they were often cut short. My guess would be that each interaction with this customer service rep greatly detracted from the value of that customer for the company.

I then visited another of the company's call centers shortly after the first. This was a different product line altogether, as well as a completely different experience. Here, the agents prioritized the customer relationship over call center efficiency. The phone agent I sat with for an hour spoke with only a handful of customers, and she conducted each conversation as if she were speaking to a friend (I found out later that some of these customers indeed thought of her as such, since they had spoken to her before). She took the time to listen to each caller; she didn't rush her responses, and she treated each person with respect. She made sure that she had met all of a caller's needs as best she could before ending the call. She was truly committed to strengthening these relationships.

Guess which call center had better customer (and employee) retention rates?

Customer-focused organizations treat customers as a valuable asset, one that belongs on a balance sheet. Each customer interaction is thought of as a "golden moment," offering the opportunity to improve the relationship and, ideally, resulting in a customer who is so happy that he or she becomes a brand evangelist. Don Peppers and Dr. Martha Rogers discussed this viewpoint in their book, *Return on Customer: Creating Maximum Value from Your Scarcest Resource.*[7] The authors write that when companies treat their customers as an asset, they take a very different approach to customer interaction. Such companies also review each customer interaction to determine how it will add to or detract from the value for *each customer*. Peppers and Rogers advocate that companies should measure the health of their customer base, as well as the health of their most valuable customers, and use the results to help drive the right customer strategy for business growth.

How does your organization view its existing customers? Companies that regard each contact with customers as an expense to be minimized will not earn long-term loyalty; instead, their customers may leave as soon as a better perceived value comes along—or as soon as they find an organization that will treat them as someone worth keeping. Companies who consider their customers to be valuable assets, to be nurtured and protected, will find they are able to unlock the hidden power of their customers, activate brand evangelists, and grow the business.

Case Study

EMC Measures What Matters to Customers

EMC is a worldwide innovation leader in ways to store, protect, optimize, and leverage information for its clients. Over the past 30 years, the company has earned a reputation for putting the customer first.

In recent years it has learned that its customers see the EMC brand identity as one of technology, innovation, and a "do anything for the customer" approach.

Interestingly, EMC hasn't always believed that its business drivers needed to be customer-centric. Jim Bampos, vice president of Quality at EMC, explains, "A lot of companies have a hero culture of putting customers first, but they don't put customers first when they do business planning." Bampos says that while "customers first" is a great mantra, having an official listening post, judging business success based on customer feedback, and implementing customer-centric business plans are strategic changes for EMC. In fact, the company just received a U.S. patent for its methodology of driving business growth through metrics and processes related to customer loyalty drivers.

EMC has transitioned the company to utilize three main drivers for business planning:

1. *Voice of the Business*, which focuses on company leaders, innovation, and technology.
2. *Voice of the Market*, which focuses on the competitive marketplace and segment.
3. *Voice of the Customer*, which focuses on customer loyalty and the customer experience.

These three drivers carry equal weight in EMC's methods for stimulating business growth. This marks a major shift for the company. Per Bampos, "When we drive these areas into the business plan, we bring the customer into the process of driving the business. This is no longer a 'hero mentality'; this is measurable and actionable."

It All Starts with Listening

EMC gathers customer feedback through a variety of listening posts. The Voice of the Customer program has four different sets of surveys. The first is the "transactional survey," which is focused on

(continued)

(*continued*)

services. Every time a customer experiences an incident or interaction, the survey asks the customer how well EMC performed. The second type is the "relationship survey," which is conducted via executive interviews with the top 300 accounts globally. The account manager nominates one executive at each client account to be interviewed by phone or in person, and that customer then suggests which of his or her peers should also be interviewed. The survey includes very pointed questions aimed at decision makers. Third, a "loyalty survey" goes to the influencers at the customer sites who work with EMC's products, services, and salespeople on a regular basis. Finally, EMC conducts a "quarterly double-blind competitive survey" (customers don't know who is sponsoring the survey, and EMC doesn't know who is answering) that asks 1,000 customers the question: How well are we doing against our competitors?

In addition, the company collects feedback and data from these other customer listening posts:

- *Voice of the Field:* What field engineers, salespeople, and executive sponsors hear from customers.
- *Customer councils:* Composed of about 100 customers who gather pointed feedback on how EMC is doing and what customers want to see in the next generation of EMC technology.
- *Social media:* What customers are saying about the industry, satisfaction, customer buzzwords, and how well EMC is doing.

The company plans to officially incorporate these additional data points into the Voice of the Customer program in the near future.

Customers Drive Growth

Although EMC's Total Customer Experience (TCE) program was already enabling the company to measure customer loyalty and metrics to help drive business, EMC determined that it wasn't always measuring the right areas from the perspective of the customers and what mattered most to them.

For example, a few years ago EMC discovered that the service response times had a high impact but a medium to low satisfaction level with customers. By taking a fresh look at this metric from the customer's point of view, EMC realized it had not been measuring response times in such a way that would result in improvement for the customer.

In another example, the company's Implementation Services Team had been dedicated to measuring budget and on-time delivery when they talked about TCE—but, again, from the company's, not the customer's perspective. Bampos said they have fundamentally changed this aspect of the program by developing new metrics that better measure areas that impact customers.

Change That Shows

EMC now tracks three separate sets of metrics: financial, operational (how well the business runs), and customer. All teams focus on metrics that affect the customer, and according to Bampos, those are the ones that directly correlate to customer loyalty and customer loyalty drivers. When EMC receives customer experience survey results, management reviews the feedback in a four-quadrant graph. The horizontal x-axis shows the impact on customer success based on what vendors provide, ranging from low to high impact. The vertical y-axis charts the scores of those attributes according to how satisfied EMC customers are with delivery, from low to high satisfaction. Each customer loyalty attribute is then mapped to the graph to help determine what business action to take. Attributes that fall in the lower right quadrant (high impact, low satisfaction) are a high priority. Attributes that fall in the lower left quadrant (low impact, low satisfaction) need to be questioned: Do they truly matter to the business? Those attributes that fall in the upper left (low impact, high satisfaction) are to be continually maintained, and those in the upper right (high impact, high satisfaction) are promoted and marked for continual improvement.

EMC then uses a correlation methodology to relate the metrics it gathers to business results. Analysts ask themselves whether

(*continued*)

(*continued*)

the metric correlates to business performance, as well as what the performance and acceptable thresholds are for customer expectations. EMC uses this information to make recommendations for improving the measurement system, and these are translated into TCE targets across the business for each function. People in each department are paid based on whether those targets are met, both individually and as a department. In this way, explains Bampos, EMC maps customer touch points and loyalty feedback to drive continual improvement throughout the organization. All three areas are used—Voice of the Business, Voice of the Market, and Voice of the Customer—to fully understand which other business and market attributes are important to drive growth, and EMC combines those results with the four-quadrant analysis to set business driver levels across the organization.

A Continuous Process

Bampos says that as a result of the new EMC processes, customers have been delighted with the changes in the customer experience. He commented, "In the areas we have focused on, we have seen great progress." However, he also notes that every time they fix one area, something else moves into the high-impact, low-satisfaction area to take its place. EMC hears a lot of this kind of customer feedback: "Thank you for taking care of this issue; now go work on that one." For example, the response time issues mentioned earlier are no longer on the company radar. A quick response time is now a basic expectation of EMC customers, and thus other customer issues have become top priority. As Bampos points out, "You are never done."

Fortunately, raising customer expectations through better execution has proved beneficial for EMC: It has increased the company's "share of wallet" with its customers. For example, the company produces a quarterly TCE scorecard for some of its key accounts, to understand customer loyalty feedback; it identifies what EMC's service performance looks like for the customer, what the revenue is for the customer, and so on. These results give EMC valuable credibility with customers. According to Bampos, last quarter, 2 of the company's top 10 accounts required the same scorecard from EMC competitors—and the competition couldn't provide it. Said Bampos, "We got some significant contracts as a result. We are winning in a lot of ways now."

Success Factors

EMC's new customer-focused approach goes all the way to the top of the organization. Not only does the company pay its employees based on the new business goals and objectives that result from this process, the Voice of the Customer scorecard is discussed first at each quarterly business review with senior executives and the EMC board. Voice of the Business and Voice of the Market are reviewed next. Bampos feels very strongly that one of the main reasons the Voice of the Customer organization has been so successful is that it is an independent organization within the company. Instead of reporting to sales, products, or service organizations, Bampos and his team report to the executive vice president of Customer Experience; as a result, his team has no bias toward any of those groups. They are free to manage based on facts derived from the measures reported in organizational scorecards; they therefore have a strong commitment to improve in the areas that matter most. And the executive team is on board because they have seen the results.

The divisions that have focused on customer-centricity to drive their business growth, says Bampos, have gained market share and exceeded revenue targets. "We can't say that is all due to loyalty and quality, but we know that is a big piece of the success." It shows in other ways as well. EMC has seen measurable results such as a 2 percent improvement in loyalty, which equates to a 1 percent gain in market share.

Next up for EMC is to tie these results to customer value. Do customers see a value in what EMC provides? Bampos states that the company plans to get a patent on this process as well.

Information taken from a personal interview with Jim Bampos on January 28, 2011.

Chapter 11

THE POWER BEHIND THE SCENES

Most employees in an organization don't understand what it takes to provide good customer service, much less killer customer service. Yet it is the employees who play a major role in making the customer service experience positively memorable. For example, among the best features of Starbucks coffee shops are the baristas, their employees. At every Starbucks I've ever gone into around the world, they are always friendly, smiling, and helpful. They know the names of their regulars and chat with them on sight. They are patient when explaining their products to newbies who don't understand (and there is quite an extensive lingo to learn in regard to the menu of coffee beverages). They always listen carefully when children are placing the drink orders, treating them as important (and future!) customers. They are polite and quick to help when there is a mishap (like a spill), never making anyone feel bad. They apologize when there is a wait, and they thank patrons for their business. They make it right when there is a problem with an order. In short, the Starbucks baristas truly help power the company's entire Starbucks experience.

Every employee in every company should be responsible for customer service. The right people, actively engaged in the company and empowered to do what is right for the customer, can serve as catalysts for business growth through existing customers. Whether serving internal customers, vendors, or clients, each person plays a role in creating the best experience for your customers.

HIRE FOR ATTITUDE

"Customers Rock!" companies focus on hiring the right employees—individuals who are naturally people-focused, have passionate spirits, are empathetic, and like to think creatively to solve problems. Southwest Airlines calls this having "a Servant's Heart, a Warrior Spirit, and a Fun-LUVing Attitude." (See the Southwest Airlines case study at the end of this chapter for more details.)

Hire for Passion, Teach the Skill

Sybil Stershic, author of *Taking Care of the People Who Matter Most*: *A Guide to Employee–Customer Care*, believes that good customer service people are born, not made.[1] Some people just naturally have a caring attitude for others. They are empathetic, good listeners, and possess a positive outlook. Good customer service people are also problem-solvers who want those around them to be happy.

Recently, I observed Southwest Airlines personnel doing what they do best: treating people as people. While waiting to board a plane, I saw a young girl, about nine years old, getting ready to fly alone. Her escort (most likely her mother) was in tears as she walked the girl onto the jetway to board. As I entered the plane a few minutes later, I noticed the young girl huddled in her seat, sobbing into her hands.

Fast-forward about 30 minutes, Southwest flight attendants were taking drink orders from the passengers. Shortly after that, who did I see handing out snack boxes to passengers? The young solo flyer! The flight attendants had noticed her distress and to distract her had asked her to help them pass out the food. The young girl was all smiles now that she was busy doing an important job. Later, she was graciously thanked by the crew over the plane's PA system. I think I smiled the rest of the way home.

Using empathy really does make a difference to people, whether we are dealing with customers or other employees. Taking into consideration the feelings and needs of others is an important characteristic of customer service stars.

These customer service champions are not always easy to find, however. So let's look at a few methods that can be used to identify the right future employees for your customer-focused company.

Look to Your Customers

When it's time to hire holiday help, clothing retailer Coldwater Creek sends out postcards to local customers on its mailing list inviting them to apply for jobs. The Container Store, a storage and organizational products company, has been known to approach customers shopping in their stores to see if they would be interested in working there. Both of these brands appreciate the fact that their customers could make very effective employees. It makes sense: Not only are customers familiar with your offerings, but they may have already proven to be passionate about your brand. What better way to ensure that your customers are talking to raving fans? This approach also works very well for commercial companies that offer complex product lines; by hiring a customer of 20 years, you gain someone with ready-made and in-depth knowledge about how businesses use these products in the real world.

Involve Your Employees

Your current employees already know what it takes to create a great customer experience, so Stershic suggests that you take advantage of their expertise to help hire "good-fit" future employees.

One effective way to do this is to include peer interviews in the hiring process. Your current employees will often have an intuitive feeling for whether or not a candidate will be a good fit for your company and customers. Another good idea is to ask customer-facing employees to help you come up with a list of traits that make for high-quality customer service people. Their list may be similar to the one that management and HR have compiled, but the fact that these folks "live the culture" daily, on the front lines, may elicit some unique insights that help you find just the right new hires.

Look for Listeners

Customer service stars listen to more than the words customers say. They listen "between the lines," to understand on a deeper level what customers want, what their issues are, and why they're significant to them. This is a critical trait, and one not easily taught.

Ask Situational Questions

On a résumé, an individual may appear to be very customer-focused, but the rubber meets the road when you listen to them describe how they have handled certain situations with customers, especially difficult ones.

Asking potential employees, for example, about a time when they had to deal with an irate customer can reveal deep insight into their ability to act calmly and reasonably. Stershic recommends listening for empathy as potential employees describe these situations—and not always just empathy for the customer. Do they show empathy for what may have been happening on the company's side? Are they able to acknowledge how others feel? Again, this isn't something that people are typically taught or modeled.

ENGAGED EMPLOYEES EQUAL ENGAGED CUSTOMERS

What do you do to keep your employees happy, especially those who interface directly with customers? They may have the hardest jobs in the company, dealing with customer complaints day after day—and this is the part of an organization that most customers touch. A company can help orchestrate the best experience for its customers by first taking care of its employee experience.

"Marketing" to Employees

"Think about it," says Stershic, "most products and services can easily become commoditized, but competitors cannot duplicate the relationship an organization's employees have with its customers." Never forget, your customer-facing employees *are* the company to the customer, so a focus on *internal* marketing will ultimately help motivate employee engagement. Letting your employees know they matter to the company will go a long way toward making them feel they are part of something bigger.

And internal marketing shouldn't be executed solely by the marketing department! Human resources, marketing, and management teams should work together, in a strategic "blend," to ensure that employees have the resources they need to successfully serve the customer. The objective should be to help employees connect to the customer—and to each other.

Making Employee-to-Customer Connections

For employees to truly appreciate how important it is to serve customers well, they first need to know who those customers are and what they need. These are crucial factors regardless of whether employees work in a customer service role or in departments that never interact directly with the customer. The more employees know about the company's customers, the better they can take care of them—sometimes by taking care of their internal customers.

Here are several ways to bring the customer closer to employees:

- *Share the knowledge.* Companies should make it a point to share information about customers—who they are and what drives customer behavior—with all employees. Why do customers buy from us? What do they think of our brand? Who is our ideal customer? Give your employees a chance to ask questions and really get to know the company's customers—who, after all, are also *their* customers.
- *Conduct customer visits.* Whenever possible, take a few employees along on sales visits. If you have customer service or other staff dedicated to specific accounts, this is a good opportunity for them to put a name with a face and become more engaged in supporting the team.
- *Invite customers inside.* Some companies have customer advisory groups that come to their offices to meet with staff regularly; other times, this type of customer meeting is conducted virtually. Invite employees to sit in on these meetings. Just be sure to let them know they have to keep their feelings in check if they hear customers criticizing their contributions.
- *Phone it in.* Similarly, noncustomer-facing employees can sit down with their contact center peers and listen in on customer calls. They can also watch video recordings of customer usability studies, customer calls, or customer discussions, to get to know how their clients feel about the company and its products and services.
- *Visit customers virtually.* Another valuable place for employees to learn more about their customers is in the digital world. No doubt your customers are talking about your company on social networks and blogs, on video sites, and in forums. Employees should be given time to be a "fly on the wall" at these sites, to learn the terms customers are using to discuss industry products and services, to discover what they like and dislike, and to find out how they prefer to interact with the company. You may find that some of your employees become so interested in these social media interactions

that they want to become part of a program to reach out to customers via these channels. Employees who are passionate about your company and love to use social media tools can make effective brand ambassadors, both online and off.

These aren't the only methods of establishing an employee-to-customer link, but they can lay a solid foundation for helping employees understand customer wants, needs, and desires.

Making Employee-to-Employee Connections

Some organizations establish internal social networks to give employees the opportunity to connect with management and to support each other. In 2008, McDonald's created just such a site, Station M, strictly for McDonald's employees (their crew). Similar to other social networking sites, Station M provides a way for the chain's restaurants to share ideas, best practices, and customer stories, as well as commentary. There is also a forum section that allows dialogue between McDonald's corporate members and the crew as well as discussion between crew members from other stores.[2]

Station M has proved to be successful in getting employees more involved with both the corporate office and other crew members. It also makes good sense for the company since many of its crew members are high school age, a group that is already very comfortable using social networking sites. Internal sites like McDonald's Station M can motivate active employee engagement and create a sense of "living the brand."

Did We Do It Right?

Taking care of employees has to be prioritized if you expect the program to make a material difference on your team and, ultimately, on the company's bottom line. In order to determine its effectiveness, it also needs to be measured.

Stershic explains that because internal marketing programs engage both employees and customers, you can evaluate them using the same metrics that you use to measure overall satisfaction and retention for both groups. You can also measure specific internal marketing activities (such as recognition programs, new staff orientation, special events, etc.)

through quantitative and qualitative means (e.g., who and how many participated and what effect their participation had on their perceptions or behaviors).

For companies just getting started with internal marketing, this practice may mark the first time that the teams from HR and market research come together to discuss the benchmarks available to them from employee and customer surveys. Companies that haven't conducted such surveys before may want to enlist the services of research providers that measure employee engagement or conduct "linkage research," which reviews operational practices and employee perceptions and links this information to drivers of customer satisfaction and loyalty.

Case Study
Nicor National Creates "Positivity at Work"

Does a focus on keeping employees engaged in the brand really make a difference? According to Barbara Porter, Vice President of Business Development and Customer Service for Nicor National, "The environment we create for our employees is the environment our customers will experience." To provide an environment where employees can succeed, Nicor National works to build an intentional culture so employees will feel "this place is different," from the moment they walk through the door.

A subsidiary of Nicor Inc. and an affiliate of Nicor Gas, a regulated natural gas utility, Nicor National manages relationships with more than 745,000 customers on behalf of utility partners and offers energy-related retail products and services to the end customers. Its goal is to help extend the relationship of the end customers with the utility companies by providing them with opportunities to better manage their energy use, control their energy costs, and offer peace of mind from unexpected repair bills.

Porter explained that creating a culture where employees will thrive involves a three-step process: (1) creating the right physical environment, (2) ensuring a supportive emotional environment, and (3) allowing for strong two-way communication.

Physical Environment

Everything about the employee environment at Nicor National is carefully planned and considered, from the colors on the walls to the inspirational sayings posted around the building. Framed pictures of all employees also hang on the walls, along with their descriptions of the company's values in action, written in their own words.

The focus on the employee environment is evident from day one for new hires to Nicor National's call center. Porter, who participates in the intake training, asks the new hires this question as a group: "What type of work environment makes you want to come in, and you can't wait to get here?" The words and phrases new hires use to describe such an environment typically include "positive," "friendly," and "supports my goals," among others.

Porter then asks, "What would be the evidence of these? How would you know they were present?" Answers include "employees say hello to each other when they pass by," "employee recognition for a job well done," and "people smiling in the halls."

Porter completes the exercise with new hires by presenting this challenge: "In three months, I am going to come back and meet with you to see whether [you think] this environment exists here. If it doesn't, what will *you* do to make sure it will exist?"

In 10 years of conducting these sessions, Porter has had only one group of new hires come back three months later and say they didn't see the work environment previously described. She called in the team where those new hires were assigned (without the new hires) and went through the same exercise. On sharing the feedback from the new hires with the existing team members, she asked them how they would change the environment. All the issues raised were immediately addressed. "We have control over how we treat each other," she says.

Emotional Environment

The second pillar of Nicor National's culture is built on meeting the emotional needs of employees. How do employees know you care about them? It starts with those on the front line and their direct

(*continued*)

(*continued*)

supervisors. Nicor National assembles photo albums for call center supervisors and managers that contain pictures of all their direct reports, to help them remember they are managing more than just metrics; they are managing and developing people.

Nicor National also works with its call center employees to set goals for all individuals at the beginning of each year. In addition to professional goals, they may set personal objectives as well, in such areas as health (e.g., lose weight, eat better), financial (e.g., pay off credit card debt), and educational aspirations (e.g., earn a certification). Nicor National's leadership team then reviews these employee intentions to see how the company can help support them during the upcoming year. For example, one year, to help employees achieve their health-related goals, the leadership team gave everyone pedometers, published health tips in the employee newsletter and on the intranet, and hired a personal trainer to present a lunchtime seminar. These initiatives show employees that the company cares about them and their personal goals, which motivates the teams to feel good about working there.

Two-Way Communication

Porter feels that Nicor National employees are the ultimate voice of the customer. "They know the complete customer journey, the experience." To capture that and return it to the company, Nicor National uses the corporate intranet as the hub of its communication matrix—but with a twist. In the past, the intranet site was used primarily as a one-way communication vehicle, corporate to employee, to share monthly themes, messaging, and customer stories. An online suggestion box was also available, but it didn't provide a way to deliver management's responses to employees.

Porter and the executive team have now instituted an online two-way conversation with their employees through Nicor National's Voice of the Employee (VOE) program. To help power the program, Nicor National partnered with Allegiance, Inc., a software company that provides solutions for strengthening customer and employee loyalty and engagement. Now part of the corporate intranet, the VOE program enables employees to make a suggestion or share a compliment, complaint, or observation, as they see fit. All feedback goes through Porter so she can stay in touch with what employees are experiencing; feedback is also routed to the executive team, as appropriate, whose members respond immediately using the online tool. Porter also uses the VOE tool to identify trends in employee responses, so that she and the team can address any problems before they get out of hand.

In addition to interacting online, Nicor National leaders make sure they meet face-to-face with all employees at quarterly town hall meetings, monthly employee round tables, and daily supervisor walkarounds.

Engaged Employees and Customers Produce Results

All three areas (physical environment, emotional environment, and two-way communication) are essential to the success of Nicor National's unique, energized, and empowered employee experience and culture. The success and health of the culture is measured regularly, based on an employee engagement survey offered to employees every time they use the VOE tool. Nicor National also takes the pulse of its call center representatives via a quarterly employee engagement survey. All of this employee feedback is analyzed regularly through the Allegiance software to gain insight and identify trends in the engagement levels of the entire team.

Nicor National uses similar engagement surveys with customers, who can submit unsolicited feedback on the company Web site and respond to quarterly "pulse" engagement surveys. Through the results of the surveys, the company is able to determine the drivers of behavior for an engaged customer. The company uses this to prioritize process improvements that will help create a better customer experience.

Nicor National also takes note of which customers are disengaged with the company and which are "swing" customers (neither engaged nor disengaged). The survey results give the company an

(continued)

(*continued*)

opportunity to correct for any disengagement and move those customers bit by bit toward being swing customers and, ultimately, to being fully engaged. The company also uses the survey results to review what is happening across the board so it can strive to prevent disengaged customers in the first place.

It All Adds Up

To earn support from the corporation for investing in the employee experience, the initiative has to demonstrate it is contributing to an increase in profits. On the employee side, Nicor National uses the VOE software to track employee engagement trends and correlate them with corporate sales and costs, to determine how employee engagement levels are impacting financial performance. On the customer side, Nicor National has found that customer engagement levels closely track employee engagement levels; the positive employee experience can be shown to have direct influence on creating a positive customer experience. "We know that a 1 percent shift in customer retention impacts our bottom line by hundreds of thousands of dollars annually," says Porter. In addition, employee engagement has resulted in improved employee performance, which in turn has led to increased conversion rates of 15 percent, a decreased cost per sale of 20 percent, and a reduction in overall call center operating costs of $1.5 million for the current fiscal year.[3] Per Porter, "It all really starts with a focus on your employees, an intentional environment, and the leadership to make it happen."

Information taken from a personal interview with Barbara Porter on January 13, 2011.

EMPLOYEE EMPOWERMENT

It's important that companies empower their employees to do what is right for the customer. As you read in the Nicor National case study, employees who are empowered and feel good about where they work can turn their own positive feelings into positive experiences for customers.

By "empowered" I don't mean giving employees carte blanche to reward every customer who complains with a discount or a free item. What I do mean is that employees should be trained to listen to a customer's complaint or problem and then be allowed to do whatever they need to do in order to make it right, without always having to get a supervisor's approval.

Setting Guidelines

Not long ago, something caught my eye behind a friendly teller at my local Wells Fargo bank branch. Another employee was preparing a chart to go on the wall titled, "11 Ways to Wow the Customer." Of course, being the customer-focused professional that I am, I had to ask about it.

My teller told me that it was a way to help remind the team about customer service, with the main goal to make customers feel welcome each time they come into the bank. Wells Fargo wants the experience to be such a positive one for customers that they will seek out the branch for their future banking activities—even if it isn't their home branch.

Most of the items on the chart, I noted, were simple, such as welcoming customers into the bank verbally when they walk in the door, smiling, and, as my teller put it, "Keeping your grump to yourself!"

This program is consistent with Wells Fargo's corporate focus on customers. The following is an excerpt from the Culture page on the bank's Web site.[4]

11 Ways to Wow

"Welcoming"
- You make me feel at home.
- You care about me.
- You make me feel special.

"Delivering value"
- You give me the right advice.
- You provide me value.
- You keep your promises.

"Following up and building relationships"
- You help me when I really need it.
- You know me.
- When you make a mistake, you make things even better.
- You thank me.
- You reach out to me.

My teller also explained that this customer focus makes the branch experience better not only for customers but also for her and the other employees who work there. She said she enjoys her job more when she is able to truly help customers with their needs. She spends time talking to them about the task at hand, and she listens to them when they want to talk about their lives. These customers have become regulars for this teller (one of them even baked and brought in not one but two cakes for the team). I should point out that the pace at this branch is a little more leisurely, so the employees have time to chat with customers, their kids, and even their dogs!

I love this line from the Wells Fargo Web site: "We're only as good as our first impression and last connection. This is all about culture and attitude."

Asking Forgiveness

Providing clear guidelines for expectations of behavior is an important part of employee empowerment. When you train employees to understand what they can do for customers, as well as what has been done in the past, employees are freed to get the help they need to turn around a poor customer experience. Employees who haven't had this training may become paralyzed when they are called upon to resolve a bad customer situation. They may wonder, for example, what they are allowed to spend on the customer to rectify the situation and whether they will suffer negative consequences for their decision.

I recently read an article about an airline employee who was taking care of a VIP customer who was forced to take a cab to the airport due to a mix-up with the airline's promised limousine service. This employee saw the customer arrive in the cab and made a spur-of-the-moment decision to refund the customer for the cost of the cab—out of her own pocket.

The customer was ushered onto the flight and made it with only a few minutes to spare.

After it was all over, the employee explained to her supervisor what had happened. Instead of being congratulated for taking such good care of this VIP customer, the employee was asked for a receipt and was told, "No receipt, no reimbursement." Fortunately, the airport manager heard about the incident and made it right for the employee.

A Job Well Done

Finding employees who do the right thing for the customer, then backing them up with appropriate recognition, is critical to ensuring that positive behaviors become "business as usual." Recognition lets employees know they did a good job, which empowers them to continue to do so. It also encourages employees to become more engaged with the company overall.

Recognizing outstanding customer service delivered by employees doesn't have to cost a lot or be difficult. Often, what employees value most is simple acknowledgment, such as personal recognition for a job well done, a written thank-you, or public praise.[5] Some companies do, however, institute special programs for those who have been recognized for providing exemplary customer service. Here's an example: Each quarter, the management team at one medium-sized enterprise selects a front-line employee who has done an outstanding job for a customer during that period. The best-of-the-best is then selected annually, and that individual receives an extra week of vacation as his or her reward.

The annual Customer Service Week also gives companies around the world an opportunity to celebrate their customer service employees. This event is devoted to recognizing the importance of customer service and to honoring the people who serve and support customers with the highest degree of care and professionalism. In 1992, the U.S. Congress proclaimed Customer Service Week as a national event, to be celebrated annually during the first full week in October. During this week, in addition to rewarding front-line employees, organizations use the time to raise awareness of the importance of customer service within their companies, thank noncustomer-facing employees for their support, and even remind customers of their company commitment to customer satisfaction.[6]

Merely telling employees that they need to "take care of customers" won't bring any lasting results if the initiative is not consistently reinforced through management actions toward employees and customers. Celebrating a special week like Customer Service Week helps to provide reinforcement to employees that the company really does "walk the talk."

EMPLOYEES MAKE THE DIFFERENCE

Customer service can be a significant differentiator for a company. This should come as no surprise when you consider that customer service is where most direct customer interaction takes place and that it's the face of the brand for many customers. Customer service can also lead to competitive advantage as you learn things about your customers that your competitors don't know, simply because you have the relationship already.

All your employees play a major part in making this customer service relationship successful, whether they face customers directly or take care of "internal customers." According to Jonathan Tisch, chairman and CEO of Loews Hotels, the following are the basic tenets for taking care of employees so they will take care of your customers:[7]

- Hire employees who display a natural warmth and genuinely caring attitude.
- Ensure that employees at all levels understand the basic vision and mission of the business, and hire people who agree with this mission.
- Institute appropriate incentives, rewards, and recognitions to spotlight employees who are doing it right.
- Ensure that management (both senior and middle) maintains a regular and direct dialogue with the front-line team.
- Listen to customers to anticipate their needs, then follow through on meeting them.
- Make the service experience consistent.

Maintain your focus on your employees at all times—especially when things are difficult. Never forget, they are your brand ambassadors to the outside world. Customers will develop relationships with your employees that will help drive additional business, as well as referrals to new customers. These relationships will also help cement the loyalty of your existing customers.

Case Study
Southwest Airlines Is Passionate about People

Southwest Airlines doesn't assume that good customer service can be taught, nor does the airline rely on "random acts of customer service." Southwest Airlines is committed to hiring the right people to make it happen. In fact, employees are hired for their attitude; the skills they will need are taught. Living the Southwest Way means having "a Servant's Heart," "a Warrior Spirit," and a "Fun-LUVing attitude." Employees are encouraged to be proactive in their approach to customer service, to apologize if needed, to make a personal connection with customers, and to put their customers ahead of themselves. Dave Ridley, senior vice president of Revenue Management and Marketing at Southwest Airlines, shared with me that it takes the right people, servant leadership, and employee empowerment to create a wonderful customer experience.

Hire Happy People
According to Ridley, it all starts with hiring the right people at Southwest Airlines. Being "other-oriented," he believes, is either in someone's DNA or it's not, and Southwest's hiring process aims to ascertain which people truly have a heart for others. As Ridley explains, "You don't train people to be happy; you hire happy people."

During interviews for new hires, current Southwest employees participate and help observe the prospects. In group interviews, for example, they watch whether potential employees are paying attention to what others are saying, or whether they're crossing their arms and looking at the ceiling. When talking about their proudest accomplishments, do potential employees acknowledge the contributions of others, or is it "all about them?"

(continued)

(*continued*)

Be a Servant Leader

It takes hard work to create an environment where great customer service happens organically, and Southwest's leadership team is deeply committed to sustaining this culture. Per Ridley, "The most important employees at Southwest are not our officers and directors. The most important employees are our people, and [we need to see] decisions through their eyes." Southwest determines the way forward based on how those decisions affect an employee's ability to do his or her job effectively, yet with passion for their work and compassion for others. By putting their people first—ahead of customers and shareholders—Southwest is able to nurture long-standing employee loyalty, which is essential to Southwest Airlines' ability to deliver outstanding customer service.

The management team also serves their employees in a way that models how the airline wants employees to treat their customers. Here's an example of what might happen on a hot day in July. As tired flight attendants prepare for yet another back-to-back flight, and start cleaning the cabin of trash and tidying up the seat belts before the next passengers board, their management team comes onto the aircraft—carrying frozen yogurts for everyone. They instruct the flight attendants to take a seat, enjoy their cold treats, and let the managers clean the plane. "As leaders, people listen to our words, but they most closely watch our actions," says Ridley.

The leaders of Southwest Airlines strive to put their employees first, which in turn demonstrates to employees how to better serve their customers.

Treat Your Customer as Yourself

Although company manuals exist for specific jobs at Southwest Airlines, nowhere in those manuals are there details about how to take care of customers. Since employees have been hired for their empathic natures and positive attitudes, they are essentially instructed to take care of each customer as if that customer were a brother, mother, father, best friend—or themselves. To achieve this, Southwest employees are given a lot of latitude in how they express their attitude to customers. They are empowered to do what it takes to make each customer's experience with Southwest Airlines a great one.

Ridley shared a story with me of a customer who left a Bible in the backseat pocket on a plane. Three days later, the Bible was returned to the customer, via overnight delivery—with an added surprise. The Southwest employee who found it had first called to make sure she had the correct mailing address before enclosing a $20 gift card for McDonald's in the Bible and sending it back to the owner.

Nowhere in Southwest's employee manual does it say to go out and buy a $20 gift card to McDonald's when returning a lost item, but this employee felt it would be a nice thing to do, and so she did it. This type of story adds the Wow! factor to Southwest Airlines, and the telling of such stories can become infectious. Southwest encourages its employees to do things outside of their job description, and when in doubt, to err in the customer's favor. According to Ridley, "If they err on the side of great customer service, and we see later that it wasn't ideal, that's okay. We want our employees to do what they believe is right without being concerned about negative repercussions."

Measuring Passion

Southwest Airlines focuses on matters of the heart, which can't really be measured. "You can't put human spirit on a graph," Ridley stated when asked about which metrics the airline uses to help drive customer service. Southwest Airlines deals with 100 million customers annually through the interactions of 35,000 employees, two-thirds of whom are customer-facing. While Southwest does review how many positive remarks it receives from customers, Ridley reiterates that it's not about the numbers. (The airline, by the way, leads the industry with a ratio of eight compliments to one complaint, and it has had the fewest number of customer complaints filed with the Department of Transportation (DOT) since 1987, when the DOT

(continued)

(*continued*)

started tracking this factor.) "When listening to a customer," says Ridley, "there may be commendations or complaints, but our employees try to listen for the *passion* of the customers behind their statements. Many organizations can miss the point of using people on the front lines to deliver a wonderful customer experience through too much focus on the metrics."

Results

Southwest Airlines puts its employees first; they are the top priority. Once it has taken care of that priority, it knows that the rest (customers, shareholders) will follow. As a result, Southwest Airlines is ranked first among airlines in the American Customer Satisfaction Index—a position it has held for 17 years.

Information taken from a personal interview with Dave Ridley on January 10, 2011.

R
O
C
K—KILLER CUSTOMER SERVICE

Consistency is key.

onsider the following scenario. A customer is standing in line at a retail store. The line is very long, and the checker seems to be taking forever. The customer feels like complaining, and he wastes no time in doing so. Via social networking over his mobile phone, his closest friends, and countless others, are literally at his fingertips.

The combination of social media and mobile devices produces the perfect storm for frustrated customers, making customer service more critical than ever for companies large and small, across all industries. It has become imperative for brands and companies to listen constantly, and beyond their normal channels, to learn of any customer service issues. Those who don't will quickly fall behind.

At the same time, customer service needs an extreme makeover. Service personnel too often are treated as second-class citizens inside their own companies. So is it any surprise when they treat customers the same way? Moreover, contact centers are regarded as cost centers, so in difficult times many of the budget cuts are made in these departments.

This shouldn't be the case! Customer service *is* the brand to most customers; the majority of customer-facing interactions take place in this arena. It's time for companies to stop viewing customer service as a "cost of doing business" and start viewing it as a key to ensuring strong business growth, forming solid customer relationships, and, ultimately, earning referrals to new customers.

Today, even great customer service is no longer enough; it's just the price of admission. Organizations that succeed in the twenty-first century will have to make killer customer service their fourth key (to complement relevant marketing, an orchestrated customer experience, and a customer-focused culture). Doing so will enable the kind of service that drives consumers to share their positive experiences with everyone they know, online and offline—the kind of customer service that unlocks the hidden power of your customers.

Chapter 12

IGNORE CUSTOMERS AT YOUR PERIL

CUSTOMER SERVICE IS THE NEW MARKETING

A friend of mine staying at a hotel realized he had forgotten his tooth-brush and so was relieved to see a sign in his room indicating that the hotel offered replacements for commonly forgotten items. But when he went down to the front desk to ask for a toothbrush, the desk clerk informed him that they didn't have any, then referred him to the gift shop, where he could purchase one. My friend shared this story the next day at a workshop where he was giving a seminar (the reason for his trip). Consequently, one of the participants, who had been planning to spend quite a bit of money at that same hotel, began to reconsider his plans based on my friend's experience, thinking that if the hotel didn't follow through on the little things, how could it possibly attend to the more important needs of its customers?

Perhaps you have heard someone say that "customer service is the new marketing." This isn't a new concept; every customer-company touch makes another brand impression on the customer, especially in customer service (whether delivered in person, by phone, via e-mail, through social media, or by self-service). Each customer service representative says more about the brand by how a customer is treated than any marketing campaign possibly could.

What does your customer service department say about *your* brand?

Making an Impact

Getting customer service right is one of the most influential efforts a company can make to increase customer loyalty and advocacy. **175**

According to a recent survey, customer service is a major driver of consumer recommendations for a company, with 55 percent of consumers recommending a company based on its customer service—higher than the percentage of consumers who would do so based on products or price. Others are greatly influenced by these recommendations, with 55 percent of consumers stating they became customers of a certain company because of its reputation for providing great customer service. In addition, 85 percent claimed that they would be willing to pay a higher price if they could be ensured an excellent customer experience.[1]

Taken together, these numbers tell quite a story. Killer customer service is more than important to customers; it can make or break a purchase decision, now or in the future. In addition, if companies were willing to guarantee a superior customer experience, it could have an even greater impact. For example, the same study indicates the U.S. airline industry could have made an additional $10.6 billion in revenue in 2010 if airlines could have guaranteed a superior customer experience. This amounts to more than five times the predicted deficit that plagues the industry today. In an industry that is struggling to recover, customer service could have a very positive influence on both individual airlines and the industry as a whole.

Perception or Reality?

What's interesting to note is that the level of service that companies claim to provide doesn't match up with the level customers report they receive. Simply put, there's a gap between company thinking and customer perception. Another survey revealed that 75 percent of executives (from 35 large consumer technology companies) felt their companies were providing "above average" customer service, while slightly less than 60 percent of their consumers (more than 1,200 consumers surveyed) were satisfied with their service. This may not come as a surprise to many of you! More importantly, the survey showed that 81 percent of customers felt they were treated poorly and would not buy again from the same company.[2]

Too many cost reductions in the area of customer service have ruined customer relationships. So why is customer service often on the bottom rung of the corporate ladder? The reason may lie in the way a company perceives its current customers.

HOW DO YOU VIEW YOUR CUSTOMERS?

Does your company view its customers as an irritant or a treasure? I was at a local office supplies store to pick up a digital camera I had ordered from its Web site. The store was very busy that day, and customers seemed a little grumpy. Knowing that customer service can be a tough job, I smiled when I approached the cashier. As I handed him the slip for my online purchase, he grunted and gave it to the "runner" to retrieve my camera. He didn't say a single word to me. Nevertheless, I tried to make small talk with him; I asked whether it was a particularly busy day. His sullen response was, "No, it's always like this." End of conversation. I felt like I was inconveniencing him, so I didn't say anything else, took my purchase, and left. A sincere smile and a "Thank you very much for choosing to shop with us today" would have worked wonders!

What does the attitude of our customer service personnel convey to our customers about how our company views them? Our customers know how much we value them when we provide killer customer service. It is also apparent to anyone watching (and *many are watching* from afar these days) that it is desirable to do business with us because we take care of our customers. Additionally, the message comes through loud and clear to our employees, since the way we treat customers is often similar to the way we treat our employees. Everyone wants to be treated with courtesy, respect, and kindness. It feels good to be recognized and regarded as special.

The Customer Is King—Until after the Sale

My family and I had been shopping for a new vehicle and had finally found the truck we wanted. When we went to the dealership to purchase the truck, we were treated like royalty. We were offered sodas from the vending machine, fresh popcorn was popping and brought to us, and the salesman joked around with us. The "guys in the white shirts and ties" were great. We signed the sales contract. Our salesman promised to send us one of those really nice key chains labeled with the car brand. We drove off the lot.

Dethroned

Our keychain never arrived (we found out the next time we took the truck in for service that our salesman had left the dealership). We were ignored in the service department, even though we had an appointment. The service personnel seemed more interested in saving money than in pleasing us, the customers. The "guys in the coveralls" didn't seem to care about our business at all.

How did our status as customers change so drastically between the day we signed the papers and the day we brought the truck in for its regular checkup? Obviously, *we* hadn't changed. What had changed was our "label." We were now "vehicle owners," who might come in from time to time to have maintenance performed on our vehicles, but we were no longer "potential buyers" of a big-ticket item; thus, we were not a priority—no longer rock stars.

Why are existing customers often treated like this—"less than" prospects? Businesses that behave like this do so at their peril; they fail to appreciate the powerful voice the customer now has in the digital world. Even those who don't share their stories online are still important, as they could be walking testimonials for a brand *every day*.

Treat Existing Customers Like Royalty

One of my blog readers shared a story relevant to this discussion about her local all-you-can-eat buffet restaurant. She and her husband went to the restaurant every Monday, so the staff had gotten to know them very well. During the holidays, this restaurant offered pecan pie for dessert, her husband's favorite. As the holidays began to wind down, less and less pecan pie was available (it was only offered during the holidays "while supplies last"). By January, the restaurant was serving the pie only on the weekends, and usually none was left by the time this woman and her husband went in on Mondays.

On one particular Monday, the couple came in as usual and sat down to eat their meal, though they were disappointed to learn there was no pecan pie left for dessert. Their disappointment turned to elation when, a few minutes later, Bob, one of the managers, came out to their table carrying a huge piece of pecan pie! He said to them, "I know how much you love the pecan pie, so I set a piece aside just for you yesterday afternoon, before we ran out." The couple was thrilled—even more so because this larger-than-usual piece of pie was served to them on a special plate, different from the typical buffet service. The manager held the key to these customers' hearts and knew exactly how to make them feel special and valued. My reader's comment to me was, "Bob made our experience great."

She also shared other reasons this restaurant was a standout: For one, the managers regularly sat down to talk with their customers to see how things were going. From what my reader observed, "People don't seem to do that anymore!" Two, if a customer needed anything, the waitstaff usually figured out a way to come up with it. Perhaps the following statement is the most telling: "They don't treat us like customers; they treat us like we are coming to dinner at their house." (Sound familiar? See the Lexus Case Study in Chapter 7 for more.)

Keep Them Happy

What do you do to ensure that your regular customers (i.e., your best customers) are happy? If your business is like most, sadly not much. Why not? Because this task usually ends up being performed by a few people who are very good at serving others and who implement "random acts of great customer service." These random acts are usually not enough to keep people coming back in the long run. In contrast, it is those companies that provide a positive experience on a *consistent basis, across customer touch points* (different touch points, different days) that exceed expectations and win the customer's heart. Organizations striving to achieve that level of customer service will surely do so—it's in their DNA.

WHERE DOES SOCIAL MEDIA FIT?

As you know, customer service is becoming a very public experience these days. The world now is privy to all the details about everyone's good and bad customer service experiences, as they're bantered about on blogs, parodied in YouTube videos, and, finally, picked up by mainstream media. At the same time, customer expectations are higher than ever, while budgets are strained. All this adds up to the need for companies to engage with their customers in an honest and transparent way. In short, authenticity is becoming a business imperative.

Social media has pushed customer service into the spotlight. Making the most from each customer interaction is, therefore, critical if a company hopes to create a great customer experience. Companies should view social media as one more way to respond to and engage with their customers. This is not to say that social media should necessarily replace current customer service channels; rather, it should be included in a company's overall strategy based on how its customers prefer to interact.

If, for example, you know your customers are online frequently, social media might be a good place to provide customer service to them, especially if they are already using social media to interact with others. How can you determine whether this is a good channel for servicing *your* customers? Listen to what they are saying on these social media sites, and then ask them!

We Hear You

Consumers expect to engage with companies via several channels, at their convenience. According to a poll of more than 2,000 consumers over the age of 18, 77 percent preferred engaging with a live phone agent, and 61 percent chose e-mail. However, those who used social media to reach out to companies wanted them to respond via the same channel. In addition, 58 percent of respondents would like the companies to respond if a comment was left for them on a social networking site. Notably, only 22 percent of those who did leave a comment on a social networking site got a response.[3] Such a low response rate is completely unacceptable and would never be tolerated in traditional customer service channels.

More and more customers today are likely to use social media as either their first attempt to seek assistance ("Let's see if the company is listening out there") or as a last-ditch effort to get attention (when all else has failed to elicit the desired—or any—response). Companies need to work *across* their organizations to decide whether and, if so, how they will serve the customer via social media channels.

A New Path for Escalations?

Customers who use social media as a channel to obtain customer service do so for various reasons. For some, it's their preferred method of interaction, and they want to do their business with a company via a medium that's most convenient for them. Others use social media because they are not satisfied with the results they have received from traditional customer service channels; and they hope companies are more likely to respond via social media because it has such a big and diverse audience.

And perhaps they are right. Dave Carroll's video, "United Breaks Guitars," detailing his poor customer service experience with that airline, was seen by millions of viewers on YouTube. The video generated much more widespread attention to his issue than any call to a contact center could ever hope to accomplish.[4] As more companies begin to use social media, customers will eventually realize that they can get a faster response via their favorite social network and may in time give up on traditional customer service channels altogether. Social media will become their main venue to register complaints or compliments.

The Right Behavior

By paving the social media escalation path, companies are potentially discounting their existing customer service channels and training customers not to use them. Any shortcomings those channels exhibit may become even more apparent as customers increasingly use social media to complain loudly about the lack of outstanding customer service.

In some cases, the existing customer service channels are indeed broken and need an overhaul. In other cases, the customer experience needs to be unified to assure consistent treatment across all interaction touch points, including social media, phone, chat, e-mail, in person, and a company's channel partners. Fast responses on social media raise the expectations for customer service in those other company channels. Even when these channels operate efficiently and effectively, they may need to be reviewed, and most likely improved, if service levels do not meet newly heightened customer expectations.

Part of the issue may be that social media responses are not necessarily in sync with the customer service organization. Social media is often managed by another department, such as PR or marketing, with a third party (e.g., an agency) taking responsibility for Tweeting or posting the company's responses on Facebook. These teams don't always have access to the relevant internal resources at the company, so they can't make use of all the information about a given customer (assuming a company is even linking a customer's social media profiles to its customer database). As a result, the company's responses to a customer over social media may not be added to that customer's history. If a salesperson or customer service rep interacts with that customer in the future, that rep will not have any idea that the customer vented previously on social media (and perhaps got something for free as a result).

Should companies respond quickly via social media, even if it causes some of the problems just cited? Absolutely! Remember, the world is watching and listening, and it is imperative to respond quickly, not only to resolve a customer issue but also to protect the brand's reputation.

Make It Intentional

We really should be asking ourselves how we want to treat our customers overall. What is our customer strategy? Most companies don't have one; instead they use whatever is easiest and cheapest (read: most convenient for them) to interact with customers. Should they provide better, faster service via certain channels? This is a good approach if a company wants to reward customers for using those channels, which in many cases are less expensive to operate. But should this better, faster service be reserved only for a company's "best customers"—those who do the most business with a company, make the most referrals, or possibly have the greatest influence on others? Treating different customers differently is a winning strategy, and one that I used with clients when I worked for the Peppers and Rogers Group ("1 to 1 Marketing" approach).

Social media shouldn't be viewed more favorably because it's the "shiny new object" grabbing all the attention; it's still just one channel for customer interaction. Encouraging and rewarding customers to use a channel that is more cost-effective is a viable strategy, if that is indeed the strategy. But if we interact with customers via social media just because it's what everyone else is doing, how will that ultimately affect the customer experience over the long term?

What Customers Want

As I've already said, we need to determine where our customers *want* to interact with us. We should use social media as an interaction channel for customer service because it's what our customers prefer, not because it's inexpensive or "cool." Companies should use whichever channels customers prefer to answer their questions, solve their problems, and, ultimately, reward them for their business and referrals. Thank them for being a part of your organization, and deliver a great customer experience with intention. When companies focus on making each customer interaction count, regardless of channel, positive word of mouth will spread.

VIRAL CAMPAIGNING VERSUS VIRAL COMPLAINING

Well-executed customer service can be highly positive for a company. At the same time, it's also easy to get customer service wrong and then see the consequences splattered all over the Internet. Social media makes customer service results more publicly visible, through either *viral campaigners* or *viral complainers*. Here are three examples of viral campaigning versus viral complaining.

> **Viral campaigning:** Customers tell their friends and family how great your company is.
> **Viral complaining:** Customers tell anyone who will listen how much they dislike your company.

> **Viral campaigning:** Loyal customers are turned into raving fans.
> **Viral complaining:** Loyal customers are turned into frustrated screamers.

> **Viral campaigning:** Spreads slowly but surely over time.
> **Viral complaining:** Spreads like wildfire.

Encouraging Campaigners

Whether your customers are campaigners or complainers depends on several factors. Here are my suggestions for motivating viral campaigners, those brand advocates who are willing to share their positive customer service stories online.

Foster a Strong Sense of Community among Customers

Social media is a fantastic tool for helping to forge a bond between company and customer, or even peer to peer. A strong online customer community will come to your company's defense when unwarranted viral complaining takes place.

Be sure to go to where your customers are already hanging out online; if they don't have a good virtual meeting spot, take the opportunity to create one online, then invite them to your "house"!

Put Together a Proactive Customer Strategy

Understanding customer needs and differences will help you figure out how to treat your customers in social media channels, based on their preferences. When done well, this can be a key competitive differentiator.

Meet and Exceed Customer Expectations

This doesn't mean doing everything the customer says. It does mean understand what customers expect and do all you can to exceed those expectations. To accomplish this, it is important to properly set expectations up front, empower employees to do what's right, and measure their performance based on customer expectations.[5]

A company that does an exemplary job of motivating viral campaigners is Zappos.com. CEO Tony Hsieh and many of his employees have been personally using Twitter to build stronger customer relationships. As a result, the company's customers regularly evangelize Zappos to others; you can see many of their testimonials, as well as their ratings and reviews, on the Zappos.com Web site. They are indeed raving fans!

However, it must be noted that social media technology is not the sole key to success for Zappos. In fact, as described by Hsieh in his book *Delivering Happiness,* Zappos loves to use the phone for customer service and branding! "You have the customer's undivided attention for five to ten minutes," says Hsieh, "and if you get the interaction right, what we've found is that the customer remembers the experience for a very long time and tells his or her friends about it."[6]

Zappos.com started with a customer-service mind-set and has since developed the type of strong corporate culture discussed in Chapter 9. Its philosophy is that one of the best ways to market is to divert advertising funds and invest them in customer service and the customer experience instead. In so doing, Zappos takes care of its customers at every interaction, making sure customers' needs are met (even if that means referring customers to competitors); the company also maintains a strong focus on marketing to existing customers. In turn, its existing customers do the marketing for the company, through word of mouth. Zappos has unlocked the hidden power of its customers.

Taming Complainers

What's a company to do when viral complaining does occur? The company's initial reactions to the complaints can stop the negativity from spreading across social media channels. Here are a few tips:

- *Act swiftly.* Don't let things simmer too long! It is important to try to contact the complainer directly; if that's not possible, respond in the forum where the complaining started.
- *Be honest and sincere.* Acknowledge what happened; don't be condescending, and show your human side as much as possible while remaining professional in your behavior. Customers are more understanding when they feel they are dealing with another person rather than a corporation. Make sure there is no underlying issue that needs to be addressed; if there is, take care of it first.
- *Keep your ears open for further concerns.* The best approach to handling complaints is to always be listening to your customers; this way, you will be better able to "take the "temperature" of customer sentiments.

USING SOCIAL MEDIA FOR CUSTOMER SERVICE—YES OR NO?

Should your company use social media for customer service? Here are some questions to consider to help you make that decision:

- *Are your customers currently using social media to interact?* Before you even consider using social media for customer service, be sure that your customers are frequenting those channels, and understand exactly which tools they are using with each other and perhaps with other companies and brands.
- *Do they want to interact with your company there?* Usually, a company presence will be welcome if customers are already interacting via social media.
- *Are people looking for customer service assistance there?* Listen to find out whether customers are trying to contact you over social media channels.
- *How well are your other customer service channels performing?* If your customer service via the phone and e-mail is poor, starting up customer service via social media won't fix that issue. In fact,

expanding your presence into social media could make your current service problems more publicly obvious!

Whether or not your organization decides to add a formal social media customer service team, you still need to be aware that customers might be discussing your company's products and services online. Therefore, as stated in Chapter 1, at a minimum make sure you are always listening to customers wherever they're talking so you can respond to them and point them in the right direction for assistance, if needed. Remember, social media can be an ideal channel for learning about and interacting with both commercial and consumer customers. It's an effective mechanism for serving customers, deepening relationships with them, and empowering them to become your company's best advocates. These areas are especially important to businesses that want to be heard "above the noise" and grow, even during difficult economic times.

THE TRUE MEANING OF CUSTOMER SERVICE

Killer customer service can't be defined by compiling a checklist of activities and tasks. And it isn't just about hiring really nice people, or giving customers everything they ask for. Killer customer service is a way of doing business that moves rules out of the way and allows people to effectively serve other people. It requires a long-term approach, and organizations that take it will find themselves ahead of their competition, with a loyal customer base that supports them for many years to come.

Killer customer service is one of the keys to unlocking the hidden power of your customers. Companies that "get it" will be capable of rebounding from difficult times faster than those that don't. They will have loyal customers who shout about how great these companies are to anyone who will listen. Companies that don't "get it" may just hear a lot of shouting as their customers complain very publicly—and then walk away.

Chapter 13

SHIFT YOUR THINKING FROM NEW TO OLD

Many discussions about customer service focus on how to answer the questions of prospects (potential "new" customers) to help them decide whether to purchase a company's products or services. Companies with a "Customers Rock!" attitude focus on unlocking the hidden power of their existing ("old") customers through killer customer service to make their every interaction with the company a memorable one—for all the right reasons.

Keep in mind, customers are much more likely to remember poor service experiences than they are the good ones. It seems to be human nature to rant and complain when things go wrong and take it for granted when things go right—that is, unless the service is spectacular, and then we remember it and tell our story to everyone. For example, after giving a talk at the "Customer Service Is the New Marketing" conference in San Francisco (where I first met Brian Solis, the author of my foreword, face-to-face), one of the participants shared a story with me about the horrible taxi ride she had coming from the airport into the city. On her way to the conference the next day, another cab driver asked her how her trip was going so far. Upon hearing about her poor taxi experience the day before, he turned off the meter and gave her a free tour of the city's highlights before turning the meter back on and taking her to the conference. She was Wow-ed by this positively memorable experience.

As I mentioned earlier, providing *good* customer service is just the price of admission today. To excel at customer service, to set ourselves apart from the competition, we need to pay exceptional attention to everything—even the little things. We need to put ourselves in our customers' shoes so that we can make a personal connection that translates into lasting memories. We need to *wow* our customers by executing on a highly developed strategy to exceed their expectations.

LITTLE THINGS MAKE A DIFFERENCE

What can you do for your customers that will add a memorable touch to their experience?

At Colorado's Beaver Creek Resort, they bake cookies! Beaver Creek Resort is a sports destination that offers golf in the summer and skiing in the winter. It's geared to vacation travelers looking for a luxurious place to hang their hats for a week. But for all the luxury, it's the little things employees do for their customers that has earned Beaver Creek Resort the Best Overall Guest Service award from the National Ski Association four times since 2006.

For example, Beaver Creek Resort has thought about each part of the customer experience for anyone and everyone coming in the winter to ski or snowboard. What are the customer challenges? How can Beaver Creek Resort help? Here are a few examples:

"My skis are heavy."

Beaver Creek Resort has staff on hand to carry equipment for its guests.

"I have never been here before, and I don't know where to go on the mountain."

Beaver Creek Resort offers free Mountain Welcome Tours to newcomers.

"I am not sure if all the lifts are operating."

Beaver Creek Resort sends out up-to-the-minute reports on Facebook so guests can find out immediately about trail conditions and lift updates via their mobile phones.

"I can't find a table at lunch, and I'm starving!"

Beaver Creek Resort's "Greet and Seat" hosts, dressed in Western garb, use radios to help guests find an open table quickly.

"Skiing was fun today, but now I'm feeling tired and a little cold."

Beaver Creek Resort has instituted "Cookie Time." Every day at 3:00 PM, as guests begin to come off the slopes, volunteers offer them warm chocolate chip cookies. Beaver Creek Resort also sponsors an annual contest for the best chocolate chip cookies. The winner's recipe becomes the signature cookie recipe for Cookie Time for a year.

Yes, extra staff is required to provide these extras. To that end, Beaver Creek Resort uses both paid and volunteer mountain hosts to help out; some jobs are as simple as handing out cookies. Altogether, these "little things" make a big difference to anyone who spends time at Beaver Creek Resort. The resort also addresses potential problems in advance, so guests can be assured of having a memorable time in the mountains with their friends and families. In short, it has found many ways to delight its customers, with the result that many guests come back to the resort every year.

Think Small

As it turns out, the little things are *everything*—like looking customers in the eye, greeting them, smiling, and carrying on a personal conversation. Such basic courtesies can go a long way toward marketing a company, store, or resort as friendly and welcoming. And it is far cheaper than paying for all those high-priced advertisements!

As you begin to think about how taking care of the little things might improve your company's customer service experience, ask yourself the questions posed in the following categories.

- Make Memories—"What do we want our customers to remember about their experience with us?"

Set specific milestones for customer service when staff interacts with customers, to help make each transaction positively memorable. While you are at it, remind customers to share their service encounters with others via their favorite social networks by posting signs and offering incentives for doing so. Before you suggest they share, however, make sure your customer experience is up to the scrutiny.

- Meet Needs—"What customer needs can we anticipate and meet proactively?"

While customers may have previously shared their explicit needs, often there are a few areas of unspoken needs you can anticipate and handle by planning ahead. If a customer regularly does business with you, be sure to understand his or her specific needs and take care of them *without being asked*.

- Remove Irritants—"What little things irritate our customers that we could avoid by implementing some simple customer service solutions?"

Listen to customer feedback, and walk in your customers' shoes (or ski in their boots!) to find out where you can implement quick fixes at customer pain points.

■ ■ ■

I challenge you to incorporate a "chocolate chip cookie" experience into your strategic customer service plan for interacting with customers. Find something you can do for your customers that makes doing business with you more convenient, more useful, or more fun. Be intentional about it; don't just let it happen by chance. Deliberate planning turns good customer service into a great customer experience, and that will bring customers back again and again.

PUT YOURSELF IN THEIR SHOES

Some of the best customer service experiences take place when an empathetic person is able to see a difficult situation from a customer's perspective and make things better almost intuitively. Having previously lived in Northern California, my husband and I have made our fair share of trips to Napa and Sonoma, in California's wine country. One of our most memorable experiences was at Ravenswood, a Sonoma winery. Ravenswood produces mainly zinfandel, a category of wine it has helped to expand. The winery offered a wonderful experience not only for my husband and me but also for our children.

At most wineries we have visited, the tasting room personnel either ignore children (at best) or stare them down (at worst). Things were very different when we visited Ravenswood. On seeing our children (both under the age of 8 at the time), one of the tasting room managers offered to get something for them to drink. He took my sons to a "secret back room," gave them each a bottle of homemade root beer, along with a bouncy ball (with the Ravenswood logo and lights inside), and then escorted them back out. All smiles now, my kids returned feeling very grown-up as they drank their root beer at the picnic tables while we tasted our wines. Because our children were given something to entertain them, my husband and I were able to really relax and spend time enjoying the wines before deciding on our purchases. The memory of this experience has remained with my family for years, to the extent that our kids still encourage us to buy Ravenswood whenever we are shopping for wine. They will likely be loyal customers for life, as will my husband and I.

The personal touch from an empathetic employee, when it can be achieved, builds loyalty like nothing else. People make the best connections with other people, not with companies. Bringing the personal touch to customer service takes planning to make the experience consistent across all of a customer's touch points with a company. Hiring the right people with an aptitude for customer service, empowering them to make things right for the customer, creating a customer-centric culture, gaining the support of leadership for decisions made by customer-facing employees, and rewarding customer-focused employee behaviors are all necessary ingredients to crafting a consistently outstanding customer service experience.

The personal touch is one of the reasons customers have accepted social media so quickly. Social media provides new tools that enable people to connect with each other, at any time and from anywhere in the world. This personal connection can help improve customer retention for the simple reason that it's easier to say goodbye to a faceless company than it is to say goodbye to a friend.

MAKE THEM WANT TO SHOUT ABOUT IT

Some customer service stories are so amazing they get told and retold over weeks, months, sometimes even years. Such stories are usually about companies that have a strong culture of customer service. It would benefit other organizations to study such stories and apply the lessons they learn from them to the experiences they create for their own customers. The lessons from the following story are about the importance of customer relations and employee empowerment.

The Question

A few years ago, I had a day to myself in Disney World's Magic Kingdom, before the start of a conference I was attending. Hoping to do something a bit different, I went to the Guest Relations office at Disney's City Hall and asked if there was room on the Keys to the Kingdom tour. All 20 spots were already booked, I was told, but the very friendly cast member at Guest Relations suggested I wait in case a spot opened up (people get sick or don't show up). For the next 30 minutes, I stood quietly in that office, chatting casually with the cast members and keeping my fingers crossed (it was raining steadily, so I was hopeful).

The Surprise Answer

Five minutes before the tour was to begin, one of the cast members told me I was going to be able to take the tour. "Did someone cancel?" I asked excitedly. The reply was, "No. But you have been so good about waiting patiently we decided we could make our tour 21 people today."

I was *thrilled!* But wait; there's more to the story. The cast member continued, "And since you have been such a good sport about this, and you have been so polite to us, we are bringing you on the tour compliments of Disney. What would you like for lunch? It's included."

I was overwhelmed. This was a $60 tour, yet these cast members had been empowered to give it to me on a complimentary basis. My expectations had been wildly exceeded, and I have been raving about the experience ever since. This was truly a surprise and delight for me. I was already looking forward to the tour, but to be able to enjoy it for free was an unexpected bonus.

What It Takes to Amaze Customers

The lessons to be gleaned from my experience at Disney's Magic Kingdom can be applied to any business—no sleight of hand required.

It's My Responsibility

In a company with a customer-focused culture, it should be everyone's job to make sure customer needs are met—better yet, exceeded. However, when certain roles are designated as "Customer Relations," it is critical that the people chosen to staff those roles be your company's customer service *superstars*. If the Customer Relations team is dealing with your most valuable VIP customers, it is vital that they deliver a positive, if not amazing, experience in each of their interactions.

If yours is a smaller organization, you probably already know who your employee superstars are. If yours is a midsized to large company and you have implemented regular recognition programs, as discussed in Chapter 11, you can look to your recognition lists for assistance. Don't save the A-team for Acquisition; put your best employees in charge of your best customers.

Entrusted with the Keys

Cast members at Disney World are empowered to "make your dreams come true." How do *you* empower your employees to go beyond meeting expectations to enthralling customers? It makes customers feel fantastic when they receive a positive, unexpected extra; likewise, the employee who delivers it feels terrific about being able to do that little something extra for the customer.

Mind you, the "something extra" doesn't always have to be a "freebie." As discussed in Chapter 11, employees are an integral part of creating and delivering killer customer service experiences. When they are given the freedom to do what it takes to care for each customer, and policies are simplified so they don't stand in the way, we can stand back and watch our employees shine.

Killer customer service really does come down to the simple things: Anticipate needs, then meet them. Listen to customers as if they are the most important people in the world. Or take one more person on a tour on a rainy day.

Case Study
Five-Star Service Makes a Difference for Salon Radius

Customer service is all about building relationships, one customer at a time. Small, personal touches can make a huge difference. Salon Radius, a hair salon in Solana Beach, California, is totally committed to the interests and well-being of all its loyal clients. On walking into the salon, every client is greeted by name by the employee at the front desk. Every guest is then offered the salon's signature lemon-cucumber water (or a glass of wine or beer, if preferred).

All the professionals who work at Salon Radius take the time to give both new and returning clients their full attention. The staff also works together to provide little touches that make the customer experience special. Clients are not merely shampooed; they experience a luxurious advanced hair treatment and scalp massage, to deep-condition their hair and scalp. And when the service is complete, they're offered a complimentary makeup touch-up. It's no wonder clients walk out feeling like movie stars.

Customer service is more than skin-deep at Salon Radius; it's a competitive differentiator for the salon. Owner and manager David Linde has made the delivery of five-star customer service part of the expectation for anyone who works at the salon. He explains, "It's important that clients receive great customer service here, since they come to us for the total experience." To create a salon experience that rocks, Linde hires the best people, instills customer service into everything they do at the salon, and rewards customers for loyal behaviors. This way of doing business is unusual in the industry, as most salons rent out stations to stylists who are in business for themselves. Not so at Salon Radius, whose staff are all members of one cohesive team.

The Right Stuff

When bringing in new stylists, Linde looks for employees who will go the extra mile for clients. He asks candidates what it means to them to give customer five-star service. Once he brings someone on board, he usually knows within 30 days whether that new employee is a good fit. Sometimes he may like a new employee personally, but if that person doesn't have the passion for customer service that is required to work at Salon Radius, they part ways. Per Linde, "It is better to find this out early than to try to make something work that will be costly in the long run."

Those who are fortunate enough to become part of the Salon Radius team are expected to live, breathe, and be fully engaged in customer service every day. The team is self-policing, due to the strong culture that Linde and the other managers have established at the salon: "The staff just knows what needs to get done, and how important each detail is to creating the best environment for customers." For example, when a Salon Radius employee is not on break and has a slow moment, he or she takes the initiative to address the "little things," such as washing and folding towels, sweeping cut hair from the floor, and offering clients refreshments so that stylists with clients can devote their full attention to them. Linde encourages and rewards this team spirit by taking the staff on field trips, doing charity work together, and going out for fun as a group.

Client Rewards Drive the Right Behaviors

Salon Radius has also instituted a program for its current clients called Platinum Reward Points. Customers are given points for certain activities such as prebooking their next appointment, referring friends, and leaving reviews (good or bad) on social networking sites like Yelp! and Facebook. The points are convertible into dollars for use at the salon and are good for hair, makeup, styling products, or cool gifts from the salon's on-site boutique. And, as Linde points out, clients aren't the only ones rewarded through the program: "The Platinum Reward Points program has allowed us to take control of the business."

Rewards of Happy Clients

Thanks to the point incentives program, more than 50 percent of Salon Radius's clients now prebook their appointments six to eight

(*continued*)

(*continued*)

weeks in advance. This helps the salon manage its stylists' availability more efficiently, and schedules are fuller than they were before the program started. A typical client comment is, "I need to have so-and-so come in and experience this salon!" Referrals are up 40 percent, many from new customers. Salon Radius consistently gets 60 to 80 new clients each month.

In addition, focusing on customer service and providing incentives for reviews has helped Salon Radius increase its visibility on social media sites. Linde says they get a lot of letters from clients stating how much they enjoy the salon; their clients give them amazing reviews on Yelp! and Facebook as well. Linde posts all of these in the back of the salon for his team to see. Since many of the letters and reviews refer to particular stylists by name, posting the feedback helps reinforce the outstanding job they are doing. Linde explains, "A focus on customer service has to come from the top. We model it as managers and leaders in the salon. We need to be active in promoting it. We need to continue reading and learning about it, and we need to be always nurturing our employees and taking care of the clients." Up to 70 percent of Salon Radius's clients return to the salon, and they bring their friends.

Information taken from a personal interview with David Linde on December 7, 2010.

HELP CUSTOMERS PLAY A ROLE

How can companies get their customers more deeply engaged and involved with them? Social media has made it easier for user-generated content to appear as part of a brand's marketing, usually thanks to consumers. Consumers who are truly loyal fans of that brand typically will be very excited to see their submission used by their favorite company; however, anyone can participate with companies in this fashion, whether or not they are loyal customers. There are countless examples of how companies use these tactics to generate marketing buzz and excitement as part of a social media contest or campaign. However, when the campaign ends, the buzz usually dies down, and the brand finds out that the new social media "fans" attracted solely for the campaign look for other contests to enter.

Customers Contribute

However, some companies have been engaging with their loyal fans for years. Jones Soda, for example, uses photos submitted by its customers (via the Jones Soda Web site) on its bottle labels. Customers' photos are first "hung" in the Jones Soda gallery online, and a lucky few have theirs chosen to appear on a bottle. No fame and fortune is attached to this activity, but Jones Soda fans love to contribute to the company community in this fashion.

How can a brand connect with its loyal customers on a more local basis? Here's one way: I spotted a sign in front of the espresso machine at my local Starbucks, which usually has information posted about an upcoming store event or a new drink flavor. On this day, however, it announced "Customer Latte of the Week: Mary's Latte." No contest led to this recipe; it came from the information this Starbucks shop has gleaned from its regular customers.

This sign did two things. One, it acknowledged Mary and her repeat business, and it most likely made her feel special. Two, it showed other customers that the baristas at this particular Starbucks know their customers so well that they can recommend the best customer-created drink combos they prepare on a daily basis.

Kudos to my local Starbucks for reaching out to customers and making them feel special.

That's the Idea

Over the past year and a half, I have been working with the team at Verizon Residential to create and execute the strategy for their online community. In the summer of 2010, we launched a new program for Verizon Residential customers: an online ideation platform called the Verizon Idea Exchange. Powered by Lithium Technologies, a leader in social customer relationship solutions, and part of the Verizon community forums, the Verizon Idea Exchange provides the opportunity for customers to collaborate with each other—and with Verizon—on new products and services. For example, when a FiOS TV customer posts an idea for improving the product, that customer will get not only comments and votes from fellow FiOS TV viewers but also responses about that idea from the Verizon product manager themselves, directly on the Verizon Idea Exchange.

Mark Studness, Verizon director of e-commerce, firmly believes in collaborating with customers for product innovation. "We know that staying close to our customers is the best way to identify emerging opportunities for new features and services. The Verizon Idea Exchange enables open innovation by allowing anyone to submit ideas, collaborate with others to refine the idea, and vote on ideas." What makes this concept so powerful is that Verizon is committed to changing the way it does product development through this customer platform. "These ideas will be an integral part of our product development process and go directly to our product development teams. The result will be crowd-sourced ideas that have the potential to make a big impact on future Verizon products and services."[1]

And Verizon customers have gladly participated in this process. In the first eight months, the Verizon Idea Exchange saw over 1,200 ideas submitted and over 400 percent growth in comments and visitors. With nearly 140 customer ideas being worked on by the Verizon product teams, Verizon has been successful at establishing innovative ways to engage with and serve its customers.

Spice It Up

When it comes to letting customers play a role, Spiceworks is a great example in the B2B space. Spiceworks offers a free set of software tools that help more than 1 million IT professionals manage their networks, helpdesks, and "everything IT in small and medium businesses." The company has a very active online community whose members answer questions for one another and share what they think on a variety of topics.

At one point, Spiceworks launched a photo contest, asking IT professionals to create images of the Spiceworks logo, brand name, or simply a red chili pepper. From that contest, the community mascot, SpiceRex, was born. Submitted by one of the members, SpiceRex (an orange Tyrannosaurus rex) grabbed the attention of the Spiceworks team and touched the hearts of the community at large. He now travels the world visiting various members (he is made of paper, so he travels light). SpiceRex has become so popular that Spiceworks plans to feature him in a series of ads, also created by community members, to tell the IT world about the company's free software. Spiceworks recently won a Forrester Groundswell Award for the way it has energized its customers and generated widespread word of mouth through them.[2]

When you have information about your customers (e.g., what they're passionate about) that your competitors don't have, you have a distinct advantage. When you use what you know about your customers, and let them play a role in the experience—such as featuring a customer's favorite latte at a local Starbucks, encouraging active customer collaboration with product teams on new products and services as they do at Verizon, or using a customer-designed mascot in your ads as they do at SpiceWorks—now you are building on the customer relationship and increasing the opportunities to inspire long-term loyalty.

Chapter 14

CARE AND FEEDING OF CUSTOMERS

A s you can imagine, it's easier to provide excellent service initially than to try to fix an experience after disappointing a client or customer. It can take up to 12 positive interactions to overcome a single negative one![1] Therefore, it is imperative to implement a customer service strategy that outlines how to treat customers as a matter of regular practice, backed up by a plan for handling situations that go awry.

THINGS WILL GO WRONG

All of us have days when things don't go as we would like them to; companies do, too. Service breaks down. Planes don't take off on schedule. An employee doesn't show up for work. Someone slams one of your company's products on a blog.

When things go wrong with customers, the outcome—positive or negative—often depends on the kind of relationship you've built with them before the problem occurred. Does your company have a history of listening and reaching out to its customers? Does your company empower employees to make things right when they go wrong? Does your company respond to blog posts and other social media conversations? Does your company communicate with customers in the way customers prefer?

Answering these questions can help to design a strong customer strategy that will help organizations weather the storms that inevitably come. It will also help unlock the hidden power of your customers when they tell everyone about the great experience they had with your company *even when solving a problem.*

Let's take a look at how to handle customers in three situations: when we make a mistake, when they make a mistake, and when it isn't clear who made the mistake.

When We Make Mistakes

Dealing with customer complaints is a necessary part of doing business. Whether our customers are consumers or businesses, they expect us to make it right when we make a mistake. This activity is generally referred to as *service recovery*; I call it "making sure your customer comes back."

Some businesses are reluctant to go above and beyond to fix customer problems or address complaints; they're concerned about setting a precedent and allowing customers to take advantage of them. In fact, this type of interaction can be the sweet spot. Research shows that customers who experience a service failure that is then handled well by the company are actually more likely to become loyal than those who never have a problem.[2]

Many companies know this, but how many actually use this knowledge to their advantage? Too many leave these circumstances to chance and hope the employee who encounters such a situation will make the customer happy—somehow.

Mistakes will be made; what matters is how we recover from them. Therefore, we need to put a strategy in place for handling customer complaints that are caused by the company. This includes addressing the issue, helping to restore customer trust, and reviewing and tweaking processes to prevent the issue from recurring.

Apologies Come First

When a customer is upset, it's tempting to try to place the blame elsewhere. However, customers usually aren't interested in who's to blame; they just want someone to right the wrong so they can go about their business. The words we use when speaking with customers always make a difference; this is especially true when an apology is in order.

I like this list of apologies put together by Yehuda Berlinger, an independent writing and editing professional.[3] Most of them were uttered when customer service employees were responding to upset customers. They are each assigned a rating from 1 (least effective) to 10 (killer customer service) and are listed in ascending order:

- "You can always take your business elsewhere." (Rating: 1): Most likely, the customer response to this will be, "Thank you, I will—and so will all of my friends."
- "It's not our fault." (Rating: 2): This is a nonapology; you aren't seeking to redress the issue, nor are you showing any sort of sympathy for the individual who's been wronged.
- "We're sorry that you feel that way." (Rating: 3): This is also a nonapology, which roughly translates to "It makes us upset that you feel that way. If you didn't feel that way, we would be happy." It also doesn't take any responsibility for the problem, and all of the blame is placed on the injured party. Be careful of any apology that starts "I'm sorry that *you* . . ."
- "We're sorry if we did something wrong." (Rating: 5): Now you're getting there, but this statement still doesn't really accept responsibility for the problem. You aren't acknowledging that you did anything wrong; in fact, you're still hoping that you haven't. You are offering an apology for the sake of appearance.
- "We're sorry that this occurred." (Rating: 7): You are sorry, but as a matter of principle you're still trying to insist that it wasn't really your fault. Depending on the situation, this might be the best apology allowed if company policies don't permit the customer service employee to take responsibility on behalf of the company.
- "We're sorry that we caused this problem," or "We're sorry that we have let this happen." (Rating: 9): This is a full apology that accepts responsibility, and this is what the customer wants to hear. Frankly, it wouldn't matter if the problem were really the fault of someone else, such as one of your suppliers; the customer doesn't care. Most people who hear these words can't help but respond with some level of graciousness, such as, "Well, that's okay; these things happen. What are you going to do to fix it?" This is the target level that you want to hit for your customer service. But for the record, there is still one more apology that rates higher.
- "We're so sorry that we caused this problem; we are really distressed over this. Please know that we take this very seriously. This is a huge

oversight on our part. I will immediately notify my supervisor, and we will review our procedures to ensure that this cannot happen again. In the meantime, that is no consolation to you for our lack of service! What can we do to regain your trust? We will be sending you a little surprise as a token of our appreciation for having you as a customer." (Rating: 10): In truth, this little speech may continue until the customer interrupts—and will most likely be followed by a few more apologies as the conversation closes.

The number 10 rated apology is notable for several reasons: It takes responsibility for the mistake, acknowledges a need for a change in the future, and looks to compensate the customer in some way (which doesn't have to be monetary). Note, however, this type of apology works only if given sincerely. In addition, the company needs to follow through on sending the token of appreciation, if one is offered.

Good intentions aren't enough, especially once customer expectations have been set! And the follow-through may turn out to be difficult if the company culture and accompanying metrics fail to reward customer-focused behaviors.

When They Make a Mistake

How you treat your customers when *they* make a mistake is just as important as how you recover when you make one. Often, customer service policies are overly concerned with making sure customers don't "work the system," so we end up failing to help them when they truly need our grace.

Here is an example of a company that did it right. For Mother's Day one year, I decided to take my two boys to a local attraction where we were season ticket holders. As we were getting ready to leave the house, I went to grab our season tickets from their designated spot. But after quite a bit of searching, I couldn't find the ticket for one of the boys. Concerned this would be a costly loss, but with my sons impatient to leave, I gave up, and we set out minus one ticket.

When we arrived at the attraction, I told the woman at the ticket booth about my plight. She asked, "Is the season ticket misplaced, or is it lost?" Since I wasn't entirely sure, I answered hopefully that it was misplaced—admitting that I hadn't had a lot of time to look that morning.

Surprisingly, she said, "In that case, we can give you a temporary pass good for one day so you can enjoy the park today. If you still haven't found your season ticket by the next time you come, you will need to purchase a replacement, for $20."

This was a huge deal for me! I was sure I would locate the missing season ticket when I had a little more time to search through jeans pockets and purses at home. Instantly I was relieved. I didn't have to take extra time to process a new season ticket, and I didn't have to pay to replace it—not yet, anyway. Most parks I've been to require a customer to pay for a missing or stolen season ticket, even though they have that customer's information in their system. In this instance, the woman at the booth looked up my son's name, birthday, and address and immediately issued the temporary replacement.

What do you do when your customers make a mistake? Do you give them the benefit of the doubt, as this park did for us? Or do you require them to jump through hoops? If you want to sustain a relationship, a one-time reprieve for a customer won't be forgotten.

When It's Not Clear Who Made the Mistake

Many organizations struggle over what rules to set when it comes to dealing with customers and their concerns. "What if a customer says . . . ?" or "What do I do when the customer won't . . . ?" Whether employees work in customer service, sales, or marketing, anyone who deals directly with customers will one day face a conflict, and it may not be clear who is at fault.

Consider the following illustration: A customer's truck was only a few months old, and fluid had leaked from the vehicle onto the floor mat and through to the carpet on the front passenger side. The truck was returned to the customer after the repair was made to fix the leak. However, the carpet was very wet; worse, it was beginning to smell. Multiple attempts to try to convince the dealership it should replace, or at least clean, the wet and now mildewed carpet and floor mats proved fruitless for the customer. The dealer's customer service manager gave this response to the first request: "I don't smell any mildew. We aren't going to clean the carpet." Finally, after much discussion and customer anguish, the dealer did clean the carpet and floor of the vehicle.

Let's examine this scenario. A customer just spent thousands of dollars on a new vehicle at this dealership. First impressions, including interactions during early service appointments, always set the stage for future business. The time and cost to clean a floor mat and carpet is negligible compared to the potential value of future service opportunities. Why didn't the dealership take care of it right away? It didn't want to accept the blame for the problem, even though a repair was made.

THE GOLDEN RULE FOR CUSTOMERS

The CEO and founder of a midsized engineering firm instituted a simple rule for his company with respect to dealing with their clients. He realized that the company needed to be flexible enough to adjust to client needs yet also should adhere to a set of core values: honesty, integrity, respect for all individuals, and exceptional client service. The founder's golden rule when it came to a conflict with clients was this: It's not *who's* right; it's *what's* right.

This Golden Rule for Customers is simple yet powerful. It will support any organization that is building customer relationships based on integrity and will ultimately translate into winning loyal customers. It is important to keep this rule in mind as we train and coach our employees to care for customers and their concerns. It is also an important rule to remember as we recognize and reward our employees for their behaviors—and not just customer-facing employees. The entire organization plays a part in supporting those employees and enabling them to do what's right for the customer, regardless of who is right.

Treat Them Right

Be open, honest, and transparent with customers at all times, especially when things go wrong. If you truly can't answer a customer question, say so; then find someone who can. Customer trust is often shaken by even the smallest mistakes, so admit them, apologize, and do what's right for the customer. Forging strong relationships will help deepen your customer's trust in your organization, but it will take time and planning. It is worthwhile!

TAKING CARE OF BUSINESS

As I mentioned in Chapter 12, customers today who are connected online often use social media to share and compare customer service outcomes, and this has brought this department back into the spotlight as a critical business function. Although customers may ultimately want to establish an ongoing affiliation with a company, they want their immediate queries handled expediently and professionally when they are interacting with someone from customer service. Regardless of the customer interaction channel, executing customer service well is a key success factor in creating a positive experience for the customer.

Solve Their Problem

When a customer has experienced a problem with your company's product or service, it needs to be resolved as quickly as possible. A number of customer service skills are necessary to succeed in problem resolution, regardless of the interaction channel. Here are seven key success factors for solving customer problems in a positive fashion:

1. *Respond quickly.* Customers want their inquiry to be acknowledged quickly, whether it was submitted via e-mail or Twitter! In fact, social media has greatly accelerated customer expectations for how fast a company representative should respond—from hours to minutes. Be sure to know your customers' expectations (which may have been set by other companies they do business with), and meet or exceed them to resolve the issue in the best way possible.

2. *Have a great attitude.* Customers are most satisfied when they interact with someone who is courteous, polite, friendly, and professional. Show them that you genuinely care.

3. *Treat customers with respect.* Most customers contact a company when they have a question about something they can't figure out themselves. It can be challenging when customers become frustrated or even irate in these situations, but the best customer

service employees are able to calm a customer enough to find a solution (most of the time!).

4. *Take responsibility for the outcome.* Customers are most satisfied when they aren't "bounced around" from one agent or department to another. They want to get their questions answered efficiently and be on their way, so let them know you will take care of them, then see the problem through to its resolution.

5. *Be knowledgeable about your subject.* Make sure that whoever responds to customers is able to answer most questions accurately, or is empowered to quickly get to the right person or information.

6. *Be a good listener.* Listening to customers helps them feel they can trust both the customer service representative and the company. Remember, customers may be giving more clues to their concern "between the lines" of what they're actually saying—so make sure to look for them there!

7. *Follow up.* Finally, if you say you will do something, do it, and then let the customer know you did it. Customers appreciate when customer service follows up to make sure everything is resolved to their satisfaction. It's amazing how many companies miss this one!

Think Outside the Script

Customer service, especially when delivered from a contact center, has become overly dependent on scripts for dealing with customers. Rather than empowering their employees to listen, use empathy, and respond authentically, many companies whose contact centers run as cost centers provide their employees with standard phrases to use when responding to customers. These responses could be used on the phone or via chat, e-mail, or social media. I have included a few familiar "scripted" phrases here:

- "We value your business."
- "How are you doing today?"
- "I understand your concern."
- "Thank you for your feedback."
- "For faster service, go to our Web site, at . . ."
- "Due to a large call volume . . ."

- "Customers are our business."
- "I will need to transfer you."
- "Sorry for your inconvenience."
- "I am not allowed to do that."

Many of these phrases are, in fact, examples of poor customer service scripts. Consequently, customers who hear these types of phrases often enough will, understandably, begin to question the sincerity of the representative. They will also begin to suspect they are about to have a poor service experience. Long-term trust may also be affected, especially if a customer has a difficult problem to resolve, if it's a repeat call, or if the customer has been transferred multiple times—"If you really valued my business, you wouldn't treat me like this!"

Emily Yellin, a journalist and author, spent time with customer service phone agents at a major airline while conducting research for her book *Your Call Is (Not That) Important to Us: Customer Service and What It Reveals About Our World and Our Lives.*[4] In it, she reveals how important it is for phone agents to really listen to the customer before responding with "company policy," to choose carefully which words they use on the phone so they aren't accidentally rude, and to regard each caller as a fellow human being.

After participating in a session with a corporate trainer talking to phone agents about choosing their words, Yellin shared the trainer's sage advice:

We've got to be careful, you guys. Because we might have heard that sob story or that person's problem a lot in the last twenty or thirty calls. But this is that person's one time—their only time—to call with it. So it's hard, and challenging. The longer we're here, the more we need to keep that in the front of our minds. We don't want to come across like we don't care.

Customer service scripts can detract from the human side of customer service employees by forcing them to use responses that more closely resemble an automated system than an actual person. Better to empower employees to be honest and speak from the heart. Companies may find they can do away with a script altogether by staffing customer-facing roles with naturally empathetic people, supporting them with a culture of customer service that allows them to make the right choices for the customer, and providing servant leadership that reinforces what they are doing right.

Tips for Improvement

"Customers Rock!" companies understand that every interaction with customers has an impact not only on their customers' level of satisfaction but also on the brand overall. If you must use scripts, here are some tips to improve them:

1. *Review your scripts across all customer touch points.* Look for overused or potentially irritating key phrases, and replace them with more customer friendly wording; or, give employees latitude to think beyond the script.
2. *Train agents not to repeat phrases that are on a script if the phrase doesn't make sense in a given situation.* This requires agents who can think on their feet and for themselves!
3. *Treat your most valuable customers with special care.* Flag them as they come in so that agents can appropriately recognize them in conversation.

FOCUS ON THE CUSTOMER

As with beauty, client service excellence is in the eye of the beholder. For that reason, five-star service is more a frame of mind for the individual than a goal for the masses. It's not about being all things to all people; it's about being specific things to specific people.

To deliver killer customer service to our customers, whether they're businesses or consumers, we need to understand them first. What are their expectations? What is their perspective, based on where they are today? What would make this interaction perfect for them? Whenever we take the customer's viewpoint, we are that much closer to successfully building a relationship with that customer—and ultimately securing loyalty and positive word of mouth. And we are that much closer to unlocking the hidden power of our customers.

Case Study
Mighty Fine Burgers Serves It Up Right

"Do you want red, yeller, or white?" may be a question you are asked when ordering up your meal at Mighty Fine Burgers, Fries, and Shakes in Austin, Texas. That's the restaurant's unique way of saying "ketchup, mustard, and mayo" and one of the many ways Mighty Fine creates an experience for its guests.

K&N Management is the licensed Austin-area developer for Rudy's Country Store & Bar-B-Q in Austin and the creator of Mighty Fine Burgers, Fries, and Shakes, two fast-casual restaurant concepts. This small business has Wow-ed its customers in a big way through its vision to "become world-famous by delighting one guest at a time." And Mighty Fine does so—through its customer service philosophy, regular guest feedback, and a crew of team members who are all passionate about delighting guests.

World-Class Service

Mighty Fine Burgers, Fries, and Shakes sets high standards for its food and service, which are detailed on the company Web site. All food is made fresh on-site, a process that includes grinding and hand-forming the beef into patties, crinkle-cutting the potatoes for the fries, and mixing the shakes by hand, all with fresh ingredients. Other little touches in each store add surprises for guests, including the special-order hand Jacuzzis in the restrooms, a viewable kitchen, and surprise T-shirt "upgrades" for customers coming into Mighty Fine wearing a competitor's shirt.[5,6]

Providing this high level of customer service begins with the hiring process. According to K&N Management's Public Relations Specialist Allison Dreiband, the company uses a system called "Top-grading" that allows managers to select just the right people for each position (a passion for delighting guests is an important characteristic). K&N Management also has a very extensive training process that incorporates the FISH philosophy of customer service (inspired by Seattle's Pike Place Fish Market[7]). As Dreiband points out, "We benchmarked Pike Place Fish Market in 2001 and tweaked the philosophy to fit our culture."

K&N Management uses the four key aspects of the model and puts them into the "Four Steps of Fish," beginning with Choose Your Attitude, followed by Be Present, Make Their Day, and Play. FISH is introduced to new hires at K&N Management's Foundations Class and is reiterated throughout the training process. Each team member is held accountable, measured, and coached. "FISH teaches team members to go above and beyond to create a memorable experience, thus creating a lifelong guest," said Dreiband.

Continual Feedback

K&N Management has several systems in place to gather feedback on the guest experience. For one, it uses an outside company that sends mystery shoppers into its stores wearing hidden cameras to film the customer service interactions. This process is used to coach team members and to collect snapshots of the actual customer experience. In addition, guests are randomly surveyed in the stores on a monthly basis. Dreiband explains that the survey is conducted on an Apple iPad; this makes the survey collection innovative and interactive for guests. K&N Management also gathers comments in the stores, on the Web site, and from its Facebook and Twitter sites; each comment is responded to personally. Managers and key leaders are kept updated on daily customer feedback, both positive and negative, with summaries delivered via their PDAs or mobile phones. All guest feedback is entered into a log that is used during K&N Management's annual meeting to help evaluate its processes and determine where improvements may need to be made.

The "A Players"

The "A Players" are the top 10 percent of potential hires, and K&N Management strives to hire, develop, and retain them. Here's how Dreiband describes them: "An 'A Player' at K&N Management is someone who thrives in our culture, follows our processes, and delights our guests. They are engaged team members who are fully

(continued)

(*continued*)

committed, involved, and enthusiastic about their jobs and their organizations. They are willing and able and contribute to company success. 'A Players' regularly go the extra mile, putting effort into their work, above and beyond what is expected of them. They increase team member retention by referring other 'A Players' to our organization." They are also recognized monthly at each location—in addition to being profiled on the company Web site—to show appreciation for their hard work. This public recognition helps other team members see what it takes to be the best for the company and the guest.

K&N Management works hard to keep communications open with its team. If anything, the company errs on the side of overcommunication, especially in terms of any changes in process or areas that would affect team members. K&N Management is always soliciting feedback from team members and encourages continuous learning in order to support its culture of quality and excellence. Per Dreiband, "Guest delight is at the center of our culture. It is communicated from day one and continually emphasized with our team members. We believe that building a culture of guest delight allows our team members to be passionate about it, and that is what keeps our fans coming back."

Results

All of this attention to quality and excellence has paid off for K&N Management. In 2010, the company was one of seven nationwide recipients of the Malcolm Baldridge National Quality Award, the highest presidential honor for quality and excellence within organizations. It is only the second restaurant group, and the first Austin-based business, to be honored with this award. Shortly after winning, K&N Management celebrated with its guests by giving away special commemorative servings of banana pudding at its four Rudy's Country Store & Bar-B-Q locations, and special commemorative milkshakes at its three Mighty Fine Burgers, Fries, and Shakes locations. In addition, K&N Management is outperforming local competition and national chains in sales; overall guest satisfaction ratings are higher than competitors', and based on a 2010 survey, more than 98 percent of Rudy's and Mighty Fine Burgers guests indicated that they would return to the restaurants.[8]

Now *that* is mighty fine business.

Information taken from a personal e-mail interview with Allison Dreiband on January 31, 2011.

SUMMARY

SURVIVAL TACTICS FOR THE TWENTY-FIRST CENTURY

Chapter 15

UNLOCKING THE HIDDEN POWER OF YOUR CUSTOMERS

W hen it comes to developing relationships with customers, it is important to take a long-term rather than short-term perspective. While individual customers might seem "small" now, they may be approaching a growth period, due to their place in their customer life cycle or a change in status (e.g., marriage, children, job promotion, retirement). A business customer today could acquire (or be acquired by) another company tomorrow, thereby growing exponentially and becoming a much more valuable customer of your company. When I was with the Peppers & Rogers Group, we spent a lot of time advising clients how to measure the value of their existing customer base, as well as designing action plans for each customer value segment.[1]

The ability to increase the value of your existing customers is a critical success factor in growing your business; this ability will be instrumental to ending the cycle of having to acquire *yet* another new customer to replace one that slipped out the back.

Ask yourself these questions as you think about how well you and your colleagues are nurturing your customer base to grow your revenues:

- *Are we focused on growing our business organically through increasing share of wallet with each customer?* Expanding business with existing customers is often the easiest way to grow.
- *Are we doing the simple things, such as thanking our existing customers for their continued business—without trying to sell them something?* Whenever I speak to groups, I always get feedback on how many audience

members say they make it a point to thank their customers, sans sales pitch. Unfortunately, most businesses don't do this, despite the fact that this is one of the easiest and most effective techniques for retaining customers.

- *Are we looking for ways to engage our customers with us so that they eventually become "evangelists" for our brand and want to share their enthusiasm with others?* Brand ambassadors can do more for sales than a company's own marketing departments.

YOUR CALL TO ACTION

We have covered a lot of ground in this book, so I think it's a good idea to take a quick look back to review where we have been and a look forward to where we are going.

It All Starts by Listening

One of the most important and fundamental steps we can take to tap into the hidden power of our customers is to make sure we have included them in our plans. We lay the foundation upon which to build our business from existing customers by listening to our customers; soliciting their input on their likes and dislikes, needs and wants; and listening to their conversations with each other when they talk about our products and services, as well as those of other companies.

Listening Action Steps

1. Set up customer listening posts or a voice-of-the-customer (VOC) program, if you haven't already.
2. Listen, to gather customer feedback; collect it from as many places as you can. Do so regularly.
3. Include your customer-facing employees in your listening process: They listen to customers, and you listen to employee feedback. These employees often know your customers best.
4. Determine the critical insights and take action on what you learn. Don't stop at sharing the information at quarterly meetings and

then put it away; share it regularly, across the company, and as appropriate for each individual employee.

Determine the Customer Point of View

We need to take a fresh look at our business from the customer perspective. Based on what your customers are experiencing at any given moment in time, their needs may change, along with their view of your business. When we see our business through their eyes, everything looks different.

Customer Perspective Action Steps

1. Identify where your customers are in their life cycle with your company. Look at it from their perspective, not from a product life-cycle viewpoint.
2. Understand what your customers are expecting from each interaction with your firm—and why.
3. Take the time to understand your customers based on their needs and the motivations that drive their behavior, rather than their demographics or marketing segment.

USE THE FOUR KEYS

Now it's time to put in place what you have learned to help your business unlock the hidden power of your customers, using the four keys. The four keys enable you to focus on your customers, taking them into consideration in all that you do. This will lead to new opportunities to increase revenues and inspire referrals from your existing customers.

Key One: R—Relevant Marketing

1. Create relevant content based on what you have learned.
2. Treat existing customers better than new ones.
3. Sincerely thank them for their business—always.
4. Stay in touch; don't cause them to feel forgotten!
5. Reward loyal customers and brand advocates.
6. Partner with your evangelists and best customers.

Key One Results

Customers will realize they have been truly heard and that they are known and appreciated by your company. They will be confident that your company knows their preferences and sees them as someone special and worth doing business with. They will feel they are a valued part of the company. Therefore, customers will be ready to buy more from you and expand their business with you.

Key Two: O—Orchestrate the Customer Experience

1. Understand the current customer experience. What works well? Where are the pain points?
2. Ensure a consistent experience across all touch points.
3. Meet the needs of each customer at each touch point. Make sure that the solution you provide fits the customer.
4. Know customer expectations so you can meet and beat them. Also know who else is setting them.
5. Make each interaction count, to increase your firm's value to the customer, and vice versa.
6. Plan the experience. Be deliberate.
7. Monitor continuously; adjust as needed. Remember, this isn't a one-time activity; it's an ongoing process.

Key Two Results

Customers will believe they can accomplish what they want or get what they need by dealing with your company, *every time* they interact with it. Each experience will be positively memorable. Customers will not hesitate to renew or repurchase, and they'll let others know how great the experience was with your company. They will be ready to convince others to buy and become evangelists themselves.

Key Three: C—Customer-Focused Culture

1. Take care of employees first.
2. Create a strong culture, including company values, to get and keep employees on board.
3. Make sure leaders model customer service, to set an example for employees.

4. Choose the right people to join you. Ensure the right fit for both your organization and your customers.
5. Get and keep everyone excited about the customer. Help employees see how their roles contribute to customer care.
6. Measure what's necessary to sustain and enrich the culture.
7. Analyze the metrics, data, and insights you gather, then take action on the findings. Celebrate the good; fix the bad.
8. Show an impact on the bottom line. Choose the best metrics and tie them to business goals.

Key Three Results

Everyone in the company commits to being in the business of customer service. Employees enjoy working for leaders who put employees first. Everyone is enthusiastic about taking care of the customer because they recognize the importance of the role they play and how it impacts the bottom line. Customers have a great experience because they interact with energized and empowered employees.

Key Four: K—Killer Customer Service

1. Keep customer service front and center at all times for all employees, customer-facing or not.
2. Make sure that everyone knows your organization views customers as its most important assets.
3. Provide service in the channel the customer prefers.
4. Determine the role of social media in your delivery of customer service.
5. Do little things for the customer that will ultimately add up to big customer delight.
6. When things go wrong, as they inevitably will, apologize, then fix them.
7. Do what's right for the customer—always.

Key Four Results

Customers will know they are recognized, and thus they will feel important. They will appreciate being taken care of when they need it most. They will be open to having conversations about expanding their business with you. They will be ready to renew or buy again and to share their great customer service stories with others. Your customers will become evangelists for your company, willing to convince others to buy from you as well because they have been taken care of when they needed it.

HOW IT COULD LOOK

You have read about a variety of businesses throughout this book—from hair salons to car manufacturers and from burger restaurants to enterprise data warehouse solutions providers. All have taken action based on the principles of the four keys to grow their revenues from their existing customers. Can you do it, too? The short answer is, yes! What would it take?

To gain a better understanding of the process, let's look at how a fictitious small business might use the elements of four keys to take the necessary steps to focus on its existing, loyal customers, and achieve growth.

Situation Summary

Joe's Coffee Company is a small organization with a few retail stores in its neighborhood.[2] It has been in business for about eight years and is reasonably profitable. Joe's doesn't carry any debt; it funds all operations from a steady cash flow. The company roasts its own beans on-site and is well known in the neighborhood. However, the brand has earned little to no recognition outside of its geographic area.

Joe's is a family-run company, sporting a basic brand name and tagline ("Joe's Coffee Company: Great coffee at great prices!"). Its logo, too, is very simple. The family wants to grow the business, but they aren't sure of the path to take to become more profitable. And competition is on the rise: There's a Starbucks around the corner, Peet's Coffee is moving in, and the nearby McDonald's is upscaling its coffee offerings.

Challenge

How should Joe's Coffee Company design its strategy for growth?

Growth Strategy

Since Joe's is local, its success so far has been mostly due to loyal customers. Therefore, *people* will be the key differentiator for Joe's Coffee Company as it moves forward, and a focus on its customers will translate into growth. Joe's goals would be as follows:

- Keep and expand business from existing customers to sustain organic growth.
- Use knowledge about existing customers and their needs to stimulate new customer growth.

Step One: Listen to Customers Joe's Coffee can accomplish this by encouraging coffee shop employees to keep their eyes and ears open, looking and listening for local social media and other conversations about the brand in particular and about coffee in general. Conducting customer surveys is another good way to "listen."

The following are some initial questions Joe's Coffee Company could ask customers to help gauge their preferences and needs and to learn about their experiences with the company:

- *What do you like best about Joe's Coffee Company?* Let's build on the good things.
- *How often do you come in? How far do you drive or walk to get here? Do you visit any of our other stores?* Let's find out if a lot of customers come from farther away, maybe even across town. Perhaps it would make sense to open another outpost closer to those customers who don't come in as often as they'd like because of the distance.
- *Do you get your coffee to go, or do you enjoy it on-site?* Let's find out how we can make life easier for our customers.
- *What do you dislike about Joe's Coffee Company?* If you could change just one thing, what would it be? Let's identify the points of dissatisfaction.

Joe's Coffee Company can also learn about its customers by observing their habits and behavior. Once the company understands why customers come to its retail stores, the family can begin to improve the customer experience. This will help differentiate Joe's from competitors, and owners can use what they learn about customers and their needs to help make Joe's Coffee Company the preferred place for people to buy and drink their coffee.

Step Two: Learn from Feedback Start by fixing the dissatisfiers. What did the customers of Joe's Coffee Company tell them they wanted to see changed? What did they say they disliked?

Choose the dissatisfiers (dislikes) that have the greatest impact on the customer experience and fix them. This may not seem like the sexiest strategy, but if the customer experience isn't consistently good at each retail store, all the high-priced marketing in the world may not make any difference!

Step Two helps meet the goal of keeping existing customers, as well as converting new customers that walk in the door to become returning customers, as customer dissatisfiers are removed.

Step Three: Examine the Experience of Different Customer Groups Different customers will have different needs. Depending on what Joe's Coffee Company learned in Step One, it can begin to consider how it might improve the current customer experience for different customer groups. By taking the following suggestions, not only will Joe's improve the experience for these two customer groups, it might also encourage customers to spread positive word of mouth to their friends.

Group One: Businesspeople

Let's say that Joe's Coffee Company has a number of customers who meet and work at its retail stores (sometimes in lieu of the office). One way to improve this group's customer experience would be to ensure there are plenty of power outlets to plug in computers. Providing free wireless Internet access might also be a differentiator. Additionally, Joe's Coffee Company could provide branded travel mugs to regular customers, especially business customers, and encourage them to use the mugs at work. This would advertise Joe's Coffee Company to other coworkers; it would also help the environment by reducing the number of paper or Styrofoam cups used at the office.

Group Two: Mothers of Preschoolers

Joe's Coffee Company also knows that moms come in to meet other moms, with babies and toddlers in tow. There are a number of ways to improve the customer experience for this group. Let's start in the bathroom! The restrooms of most retail coffee establishments are lacking a critical element for this customer category: baby-changing tables. Additionally, offering kid friendly menu items—such as juice and animal crackers, along with hot drinks at a kid friendly temperature—could go a long way toward giving these young future customers something to keep them occupied while their moms take a break and visit with each other. The word should spread fairly quickly to other moms that Joe's Coffee Company is a great place to take their little ones.

Step Three helps meet the objective of increasing business from existing customers as the customer experience is tailored to their needs.

Step Four: Find Other Ways to Build on Existing Relationships   Joe's current customers can help provide opportunities for expanding the business in the local community. Here are a few ideas:

- *Get to know customers well, and treat them like good friends.* A friendly, hometown attitude is sure to draw a local following, which, thanks to positive word of mouth, could spill over and bring in new customers. Joe's Coffee Company might even host a party to thank customers, offering coffee samples and treats, as well as music and door prizes.

  Joe's might also find out who its most active online evangelists are and post their social media profile pictures by the registers so employees recognize them when they come in and can thank them personally for spreading the word. Joe's could also encourage regulars to bring their friends along, perhaps by handing out two-for-one "bring a friend" certificates for a future purchase.
- *Reach out to the local community.* Find out where existing customers are already involved (e.g., soccer leagues, business associations) and help make their lives easier. For example, because many soccer leagues have 8:00 AM games on Saturdays, Joe's Coffee Company

could set up a coffee station on the playing fields as a convenience for those parents who don't have time to grab their eye-opening cup of joe on their way to the game. Joe's might also hand out coupons for the "coffee box" (a large amount of coffee in a portable container), which would encourage customers to come in to Joe's and buy one to take to their coworkers during the week. The same "on-the-field" approach could work at baseball games, swim meets, or cricket matches (tea, anyone?). Joe's Coffee Company might sponsor local youth sports teams (an especially good idea if loyal customers have children on the team). If there is space at one of the retail stores, Joe's could even provide a community meeting room.

■ ■ ■

All of these ideas build on existing customer relationships and motivate regulars to tell their friends about the company. They also give customers an opportunity to share Joe's delicious coffee off-premises, thus increasing the potential for positive word of mouth.

Step Four helps Joe's Coffee Company meet the twofold goal of growing existing customers and bringing in new customers, by using existing customers as ready-made "salespeople."

Conclusion

Joe's Coffee Company has a bright future. It's already profitable, it is locally known, and it has a core group of loyal customers from which to build. By taking time to understand the needs of its best customers and determine how to improve the customer experience, Joe's will be laying the foundation necessary to sustain and grow its business from each existing customer, as well as bringing in new customers via word of mouth and customer advocacy.

NOW IT'S YOUR TURN

Growing your business from existing customers is a winning strategy. Doing so efficiently requires that you take all four keys in hand to unlock the hidden power of your customers—increased revenue. Note that any key that doesn't function properly will diminish your ability to succeed. What does this mean for your business?

- Hire people with a passion for customer service.
- Sustain a culture to nurture employees.
- Market to your customers in a way that is meaningful to them.
- Maintain the excellence of the experience.
- Make each touch point a great interaction.
- Measure everything, to ensure that you make the impact you planned, based on your business goals.
- Provide customer service that *rocks*.

By focusing on existing customers and using the four keys, you will nurture powerful evangelists for your company. Once you have them, enlist them to help you bring in new, like-minded clients through referrals. By now, you should have a very accurate picture of what your best customers look and act like. Take that knowledge and go out and prospect in the areas where you can find more customers like them.

Additional resources to support you are available at http://customersrock.net. There you'll find checklists to assist you in managing the details of your journey toward achieving customer focus, audits to help gauge your progress, and other free materials to support you with new ideas. You can also get in touch with me there as well as fellow customer-focused professionals. Please keep me informed of your progress; I can't wait to hear about your success!

Notes

Introduction

1. *The American Heritage New Dictionary of Cultural Literacy, Third Edition* (Houghton Mifflin Company, 2005), accessed February 3, 2011, http://dictionary .reference.com/browse/A bird in the hand is worth two in the bush.

Chapter 1

1. Jon Gertner, "From 0 to 60 to World Domination," *New York Times*, February 18, 2007, www.nytimes.com/2007/02/18/magazine/18Toyota.t.html?ei=5090& en=27f821bf31ad515b&ex=1329454800&partner=rssuserland&emc=rss&page wanted=all.
2. Andrew McInnes, "Customers' Problems Are Companies' Loyalty-Building Opportunities," in *Customer Experience Professionals*, a blog by Forrester Research, December 6, 2010, http://blogs.forrester.com/andrew_mcinnes/10-12-06- customers_problems_are_companies_loyalty_building_opportunities.

Chapter 2

1. IMDB.com—The Internet Movie Database. *Big*, 1988, accessed December 7, 2010, www.imdb.com/title/tt0094737/quotes.
2. Lloyd Bradley, "The New Rules of Gaming," *Design Council Magazine*, Issue 2, 2007, www.designcouncil.org.uk/publications/design-council-magazine-issue-2/ the-new-rules-of-gaming.
3. "Benefits of Right-Selling Methods," *New York Times*, June 18, 1922, http://query .nytimes.com/gst/abstract.html?res=FA091EF7385D14738DDDA10994DE405B 828EF1D3#.

Chapter 3

1. Cone Research, 2010 Consumer New Media Study, November 2, 2010, www.coneinc.com.

2. Charlene Li and Josh Bernoff, *Groundswell: Winning in a World Transformed by Social Technologies* (Watertown, MA: Harvard Business School Press, 2008).

3. "Sanuk to Release Carpe DM in Honor of Matt Sloan," in *Sanuk Blog,* July 2, 2010, www.sanukblog.com/2010/07/sanuk-to-release-carpedm-in-honor-of-matt-sloan.

4. In *RoadBurn,* a blog by FreshBooks, March 26, 2008, http://roadburn .freshbooks.com.

Chapter 4

1. CMO Council, "The Leaders in Loyalty: Feeling the Love from the Loyalty Clubs," January 25, 2010, www.cmocouncil.org.

2. Philipp Schmitt, Bernd Skiera, and Christophe Van den Bulte, "Referral Programs and Customer Value," American Marketing Association *Journal of Marketing,* Vol. 75, No. 1, January 2011.

3. Dr. Gary Chapman, *The 5 Love Languages: The Secret to Love That Lasts* (Chicago, IL: Northfield Publishing, 2010).

4. CMO Council, "The Leaders in Loyalty."

Chapter 5

1. Bruce D. Temkin, "Customer Experience Boosts Revenue," Forrester Research, June 22, 2009 (updated May 4, 2010), www.forrester.com/rb/Research/customer_experience_boosts_revenue/q/id/54750/t/2.

2. "2009 Gartner & 1to1 Customer Award Winners: New Media," *1to1 Magazine,* Fall Issue, 1to1 Media, September 15, 2009, www.1to1media.com/view.aspx? DocID=31841.

Chapter 6

1. Jonah Lehrer, "The Frontal Cortex," in *The Science Blogs,* December 21, 2006, http://scienceblogs.com/cortex/2006/12/proustian_hotels.php.

Chapter 7

1. Right Now Technologies and Harris Interactive, "2010 Customer Experience Impact Report," October 10, 2010, http://communities.rightnow.com/files/e1c8b93613/2010_RightNow_CEI_Report_Final.pdf.

2. Incentive Performance Center, "Incentives and the Automotive Industry," accessed December 20, 2010, www.incentivecentral.org/business_motivation/whitepapers/incentives_and_the_automotive_industry.2000.html.

3. J.D. Power and Associates Reports, "Drop-In Customers Report Greater Satisfaction with Dealer Service Than Customers Who Make Appointments," July 19, 2007, http://businesscenter.jdpower.com/news/pressrelease.aspx? ID=2007112.

Chapter 8

1. Donald N. Sull, Alejandro Ruelas-Gossi, and Martin Escobari, "What Developing-World Companies Teach Us About Innovation," *Harvard Business School Working Knowledge* newsletter, January 26, 2004, http://hbswk.hbs.edu/item/3866.html.

KEY THREE

1. Dictionary.com, *Collins English Dictionary—Complete & Unabridged 10th Edition* (HarperCollins Publishers), accessed January 7, 2011, http://dictionary.reference.com/browse/culture.
2. Felicia Bergeron and David Wyld, "Top Ten Management on Corporate Culture: An Overview of Why Businesses Do What They Do??" November 28, 2010, http://bizcovering.com / management/ top-ten-management-on-corporate-culture-an-overview-of-why-businesses-do-what-they-do.

Chapter 9

1. Bill Marriott, "A Marriott Associate Who Gave the Pants Off His Legs," in *Marriott on the Move* blog, April 2, 2009, www.blogs.marriott.com/marriott-on-the-move/2009/04/a-marriott-associate-who-gave-the-pants-off-his-legs.html.
2. www.Nordstrom.com.
3. David Packard, *The HP Way: How Bill Hewlett and I Built Our Company* (New York: HarperCollins, 1995).
4. Tony Hsieh, *Delivering Happiness: A Path to Profits, Passion, and Purpose* (New York: Business Plus, June 2010), pp. 155–159.
5. Jeanne Bliss, *Chief Customer Officer: Getting Past Lip Service to Passionate Action* (San Francisco: Jossey-Bass, 2006).

Chapter 10

1. Information taken from a personal interview with Esteban Kolsky on January 14, 2011.
2. Sarah Simon, "Linking Business Performance Metrics with Survey Data," in *Allegiance Blog*, November 1, 2010, http://blog.allegiance.com/2010/11/linking-business-performance-metrics-with-survey-data.
3. Information taken from a personal interview with Chris Cottle on January 19, 2011.
4. Net Promoter, accessed December 18, 2010, www.netpromoter.com/np/index.jsp.
5. Information taken from a personal interview with Janet LeBlanc on January 19, 2011.
6. The author, *Metrics for Social Customer Service*—an eBook, edited by Esteban Kolsky. The Social Customer, November 15, 2010, http://thesocialcustomer.com.

7. Don Peppers and Martha Rogers, PhD, *Return on Customer: Creating Maximum Value from Your Scarcest Resource* (New York: Crown Business, 2005).

Chapter 11

1. Sybil F. Stershic, *Taking Care of the People Who Matter Most: A Guide to Employee-Customer Care* (Rochester, NY: WME Books, 2007), p. 11.
2. Heather Oldani and Steve Wilson, "BlogWell Minneapolis Social Media Case Study, McDonald's," August 13, 2009, www.slideshare.net/GasPedal/blog-well-msp-mc-donalds-v25.
3. "Allegiance Nicor National Case Study," Allegiance, Inc., 2010, www.allegiance .com/documents/Allegiance_Nicor_National_Case_Study.pdf.
4. Wells Fargo Bank, "11 Ways to Wow!," accessed December 7, 2010, www .wellsfargo.com/invest_relations/vision_values/7.
5. Stershic, *Taking Care of the People Who Matter Most*, p. 29.
6. Customer Service Week Web Site, accessed December 4, 2010, www.csweek .com/customer_service_week.php.
7. "Jonathan Tisch Answers Reader Questions," interview with Jonathan Tisch, June 4, 2007, http://customersrock.wordpress.com/2007/06/04/jonathan-tisch-answers-reader-questions.

Chapter 12

1. RightNow Technologies, "Customer Experience Report: North America October 10, 2010."
2. Bob Sullivan, "CEOs Think Customer Service Is Great," MSNBC. May 22, 2007, http://redtape.msnbc.com/2007/05/ever_wonder_why.html.
3. RightNow Technologies, Customer Experience Report.
4. Dave Carroll, "United Breaks Guitars," July 6, 2009, www.youtube.com/watch?v=5YGc4zOqozo.
5. The author, "Does Social Media Help or Hurt Customer Service?" *The Social Customer*, January 15, 2011, http://thesocialcustomer.com.
6. Tony Hsieh, *Delivering Happiness: A Path to Profits, Passion, and Purpose* (New York: Business Plus, 2010), p. 142.

Chapter 13

1. Personal interview with Mark Studness, Verizon Director of E-commerce.
2. Forrester Groundswell Awards, "Spiceworks Users Spread the Word and Create SpiceRex—Who Says Business Users Can't Be Social?," September 13, 2010, http://groundswelldiscussion.com/groundswell/awards2010/detail.php ?id=381.

Chapter 14

1. Amy Smith and Ruth Bolton, "An Experimental Investigation of Customer Reactions to Service Failure and Recovery Encounters: Paradox or Peril?" p. 1, accessed January 10, 2011, www.ruthnbolton.com/Publications/PARADOXFV.pdf.
2. Smith and Bolton, "An Experimental Investigation of Customer Reactions to Service Failure and Recovery Encounters: Paradox or Peril?" p. 18.
3. Yehuda Berlinger, "Ethics in Gaming 6.0," June 2006, www.thegamesjournal .com/articles/Ethics6.shtml.
4. Emily Yellin, *Your Call Is (Not That) Important to Us: Customer Service and What It Reveals About Our World and Our Lives* (New York: Free Press, 2010), p. 111.
5. Francisco Vara Orta, "Mighty Fine Shares Recipe for Success," *Austin Business Journal Entrepreneur,* December 10, 2010, http://abjentrepreneur.com/news/ 2010/12/mighty-fine-owners-share-recipe-for.html.
6. YouTube, "Mighty Fine-atics—Upgrade 1," May 28, 2010, www.youtube.com/ watch?v=41C2gM7mz-g.
7. Stephen C. Lundin, PhD, John Christensen, and Harry Paul, *Fish! A Remarkable Way to Boost Morale and Improve Results* (New York: Hyperion, 2000).
8. "Baldrige Performance Excellence Program: Award Recipient Profile, K&N Management," November 23, 2010, www.nist.gov/baldrige/award_recipients/ k-n-management_profile.cfm.

Chapter 15

1. Don Peppers and Martha Rogers, PhD, *Return on Customer: Creating Maximum Value from Your Scarcest Resource* (New York: Crown Business, 2005).
2. Inspired by "Growing the Business: Coffee House Blues," in "Customers Rock!" blog, June 10, 2007, http://customersrock.net/2007/06/10/growing-the-business-coffee-house-blues.

Additional Resources

The Customer Respect Group (http://www.customerrespect.com): This is an excellent resource for understanding how customers view their online experiences in various industries. Its industry reports provide summaries and rankings of large companies by industry.

The Social Customer (http://thesocialcustomer.com): This is a moderated online community for social CRM and customer service professionals. Visit and contribute.

Sybil F. Stershic: On pages 14–15 of Stershic's book, *Taking Care of the People Who Matter Most, A Guide to Employee-Customer Care* (WME Books, 2007), you will find a useful internal marketing miniaudit.

Index